GUIDED DAILY MEDITATION FOR BEGINNERS

An essential guide to reduce stress, improve your body and mental health and be at peace with yourself.

By
Rajesh Chodron

Table of Contents

INTRODUCTION TO MEDITATION, LIFE CHANGING BENEFITS 1

NEARLY THERE... 14

CHAPTER ONE: HOW MEDITATION WORKS 18

Long haul Lifestyle Changes to Help You Stay Calm 37

CHAPTER TWO: THE IMPORTANCE OF A RIGHT WAY TO BREATHE 52

A Better Way to Breathe 61

CHAPTER THREE: BEING PRESENT TO THE MOMENT, FEEL THE SPACE AROUND YOU 69

CHAPTER FOUR: BEST MEDITATION TECHNIQUES..84

CHAPTER FIVE: THE MOST EFFECTIVE METHOD TO START TO MEDITATE............92

CHAPTER SIX: GETTING READY FOR MEDITATION 108

CHAPTER SEVEN: BEST MEDITATION POSITIONS 124

CHAPTER EIGHT: ARRIVING AT A MEDITATIVE STATE 137

CHAPTER NINE: KEEPING UP THE MEDITATIVE STATE, COMMON BEGINNERS MISTAKES 147

CHAPTER TEN: UTILIZE YOUR BREATHE TO CALM YOUR MIND AND MASTER YOUR EMOTIONS.. 156

CHAPTER ELEVEN: CONSCIOUSNESS OF YOUR BODY AND ENVIRONMENT AROUND YOU... 164

CHAPTER TWELVE: STOMACH BREATHE RELAXATION 191

CHAPTER THIRTEEN: 5 MINUTE GUIDED RELAXATION 199

CHAPTER FOURTEEN: 10 MINUTE GUIDED RELAXATION 205

CHAPTER FIFTEEN: 15 MINUTE GUIDED RELAXATION..214

CHAPTER SIXTEEN: 20 MINUTE GUIDED RELAXATION..221

6 Effective 20-Minute Guided Meditations.................221

TIPS AND CONCLUSION...............................225

INTRODUCTION TO MEDITATION, LIFE CHANGING BENEFITS

Reflection is one of the extraordinary eastern practices that has begun to grab hold in western culture. Indeed, individuals everywhere throughout the world are profiting by it, both as a main priority and body. All in all, for what reason isn't everybody pondering? It may be the case that not every person is aware of all the astounding advantages like expanded unwinding, and diminished degrees of nervousness and melancholy. This article contains an overview of just a portion of the numerous advantages of reflection and a lot of guidelines for beginning your own contemplation practice.

This article is part of two principle areas. To begin with, we talk about the advantages of contemplation. From that point forward, we talk about how you can begin your own contemplation practice. On the off chance that you don't know about the numerous advantages of reflection, we prescribe you read through the following segment. It will rouse you to stay with your training. On the off chance that you definitely know the advantages of reflection, don't hesitate to avoid forward.

Advantages OF MEDITATION

There have been numerous investigations performed on contemplation in the most recent decade attempting to comprehend its belongings, just as how it figures out how to help us such a great amount of, both as a top priority and body.

An examination into reflection has shown that thinking for a brief span expands alpha waves, which makes us feel progressively loose, while at the same time diminishing our sentiments of nervousness and wretchedness. Alpha waves course through cells in the mind's cortex, where we process tangible data. These waves help smother insignificant or diverting tangible data, enabling us to center. The more alpha waves we have, the better we center.

Reflection has numerous medical advantages. Strikingly, an expanded capacity to center permits the individuals who experience the ill effects of ceaseless agony to facilitate their torment, by deciding not to concentrate on it. It can likewise help with different other medical issues, including uneasiness, discouragement, stress, sleep deprivation, HIV/AIDS and malignancy. It can likewise improve the body's invulnerable framework, making us less inclined to become ill.

Studies have likewise demonstrated that contemplation can switch coronary illness. In the diary

Stroke, 60 African/Americans experiencing a solidifying of the veins were approached to pondered for 6-9 months. The individuals who ruminated demonstrated an outstanding abatement in the thickness of their vein dividers. The individuals who didn't think demonstrated an expansion in thickness. The ends were very emotional. Contemplation offers a potential 11% reduction in danger of having a respiratory failure, and 8-15% decline in the danger of having a stroke.

Reflection benefits our psyches too. It instructs us to all the more likely control our considerations. This enables us to calm those pestering negative considerations we may have every now and then.

A recent report, titled "Mental Training Affects Distribution of Limited Brain Resources" in PLOS Biology, proposes that regular contemplation prompts longer abilities to focus.

Another report, titled "Guideline of the neural hardware of feeling by sympathy contemplation: impacts of meditative aptitude" in PLOS One, found that the individuals who reflected had more grounded levels in zones of the mind attached to compassion.

Through contemplation, we increase better focus, suddenness and imagination, satisfaction and significant serenity. On-screen characters experience the impacts of contemplation on inventiveness direct during acting classes. At whatever point they utilize their innovative driving forces, they initially ponder. It might appear to be odd from the outset, however, the outcomes are astonishing. Imagination floods to the surface once the psyche is cleared of messiness.

At long last, reflection can assist us with discovering our motivation throughout everyday life. By turning our consideration inwards, and concentrating simply without anyone else being for significant stretches of time, contemplation can assist us with increasing another point of view at life, unhindered by our own self absorbed viewpoint. On the off chance that you need to pose the philosophical inquiry, "Who am I? " there is no preferred path over contemplation.

Enough, however, about the numerous advantages of contemplation. There are numerous different sites that depict contemplation and how it can support you. How about we start figuring out how to do it.

BEGINNING MEDITATION

There is nobody approach to reflect. As groundwork for the procedure, start by relinquishing any desires you may have. For the initial not many occasions, simply sit easily on the ground, on a cushion, or in a seat, and endeavor to calm your brain. You will most likely have numerous musings twirling through your head; about the clothing, supper, cash, the children, school, the end of the week, and so forth. Try not to battle and battle against your considerations. They are flawlessly regular. As they cross your thoughts, notice them, acknowledge them, and afterward delicately bring your concentration and consideration back. You will get a progressively definite clarification in a minute. The more you stay aware of your reflection (not in one sitting, however through a mind-blowing span), the more you can calm your contemplations, quiet your psyche, and core interest.

We currently endeavor to respond to certain inquiries we envision from you.

What would it be advisable for me to feel like after I've contemplated?

Most likely you need to know whether you're "doing it right". Most apprentices feel a similar way. It is entirely expected to think about whether you are sitting accurately, or breathing effectively, or concentrating on the best thing. At last, none of those issues. On the off chance that you feel better in the wake of pondering, you're presumably doing it right.

Is it hard?

It truly isn't, the length of you don't have any desires going in. Try not to hope to sit in immaculate quietness your first time through. It's impeccably fine in the event that you don't. Contemplation is for you, and for only you. It is special to you. Leave it alone anything that it is, only for you.

At the point when you first beginning ruminating, you may battle to quietness all the internal jabber you have going on in your brain starting with one minute then onto the next. We as a whole encounter this battle. You are not the only one. The stunt isn't to battle against it, yet just to acknowledge it as a feature of who you are currently, and that you are essentially experiencing an individual change. With time, you will figure out how to quiet your psyche. There is nothing you have to improve. There is no compelling reason to attempt to speed things up. In the event that you contemplate each day, that is sufficient (regardless of whether it's just for 10 minutes).

What position should my body be in for reflection?

You can ponder from multiple points of view. You can sit on the floor, on a pad, or in a seat. You can rests, or stand up, or even stroll around! A few priests really contemplate while strolling. Spot yourself in totally any position you need that is generally agreeable for you.

In what capacity would it be a good idea for me to inhale during reflection?

Inhale typically. On the off chance that you can, inhale utilizing your stomach, which means the air will arrive at the extremely base of your lungs. This is known as diaphragmatic relaxation. It is an extraordinary instrument for vocalists. To know whether you're breathing this way, your stomach should push out and afterward sink back in. You are allowed to inhale anyway you like, however diaphragmatic taking all by itself is extremely unwinding and recuperating. It might appear to be awkward from the outset, yet as your stomach increments in quality (it's a muscle), it will get simpler. The individuals who practice yoga will be exceptionally acquainted with this type of relaxing. Additionally, on the off chance that you need to see it practically speaking, youngsters inhale along these lines normally, particularly coddles.

You can work on breathing utilizing your stomach by laying on the ground, setting your hand(s) over your stomach, and attempting to push your hand up by breathing profoundly into your tummy. That will give you a sense of what it feels like, and you would then be able to move your situation as you see fit and attempt to mirror it. In any case, don't fuss on the off chance that you can't continue it while ruminating. Everything will occur voluntarily.

On the off chance that you yawn during reflection, don't stress. It's a consummately characteristic. At the point when we do a great deal of profound breathing and enter a casual express, the body yawns normally. Try not to battle it or think inadequately about your capacity to center.

Would it be a good idea for me to close my eyes, or keep them open?

Whichever you pick. Remember that the training doesn't include really nodding off. You are attempting to stay cautious and maintain your concentration and consideration. In the event that you are resting, you are doing not one or the other (and you may fall over, except if you're resting). You can't keep your eyes totally open, ordinarily, due to residue and so forth, and our eyes normally get dry. You should flicker, at any rate. You may wish to keep your eyes shut, in light of the fact that it centers around what's going on inside your body.

What Do I Do With My Hands?

There are various convictions here, and it is hazy whether any method is superior to another. In the event that you hold to specific convictions, at that point holding explicit shapes with your hands, or putting them in various positions, will have various impacts. You are allowed to look around at the different conceivable outcomes, in case you're intrigued.

The essential methodology is to put your lower arms or the backs of your hands over your knees (in case you're perched on the floor), palms up, thumb and wring-finger contacting. Another mainstream position is to sit with your hands in your lap, making an oval shape. The rear of your correct hand sits in the palm of your left, fingers over fingers, and the two thumbs delicately contact one another, shaping the oval.

Honestly, any position will do. Spot your hands on your knees on the off chance that you like. Most want to have the hands looking up.

Where would it be advisable for me to think?

Pick someplace calm where you won't be upset. Contemplation requires a delayed center, and if your consideration is always being hauled somewhere else, it will be hard to do until you have more understanding. With time, your center will arrive at a point where you can reflect anyplace.

When would it be a good idea for me to rehearse?

Most books and specialists recommend ruminating toward the beginning of the day when our brain is completely alert. It will assist you with focusing, and you'll be more averse to get sluggish. In the event that it doesn't accommodate your timetable to rehearse in the first part of the day, at that point do it at night. Ruminating has such a large number of advantages to maintain a strategic distance from it since you can't do it at the "perfect" time.

NEARLY THERE

Since you've made sense of how your body needs you to sit, and what feels normal to you for your reflection, we layout the essential strides to make you go. It is accepted that you as of now have a period and a spot you will ponder that is peaceful, where you won't be upset.

1. Set a clock for 10-15 minutes, contingent upon to what extent you need to contemplate for. You ought not to ponder for longer than 15 minutes for your initial not many occasions. The clock will prevent you from being occupied and stressing over the progression of time. Attempt to have a clock

that signals delicately, as you may turn out to be increasingly touchy to the commotion.

2. Start your clock, and afterward get settled.

3. Begin by concentrating on your breath. Become mindful of how it moves easily all through your body. Concentrate on it, and the focuses where it changes from breathing in to breathe out. Envision that your breath is moving all through a structure, its entryway opening in the two headings and never truly shutting.

4. You will see contemplations fly into your head once in a while, maybe regularly from the outset. Your brain has a specific back and forth movement to it. Acknowledge it, and acknowledge yourself. Your brain and body both comprehend what they're doing. Recognize the thought(s), and afterward, take your concentration back to your breath.

5. If you like, you may check your breath. Start by checking each breath in and breathes out as one tally, independently. Attempt to get to

ten. On the off chance that your mind strays, start tallying back at one after you've concentrated back on your breath. At the point when you get to ten, start again at one.

6. Once you've gotten to ten a couple of times, attempt to tally each breathe in and breathe out together as only one check. Once more, attempt to get to ten as depicted in stage 5.

7. If you get to ten commonly during stage 6, attempt to concentrate simply on your breath and your body and quit checking. Try not to stress if this appears to be outlandish. It requires some investment, and you will arrive.

That is it! The more frequently you ruminate, the more rapidly you will see its advantages. You will see that before long, you can without much of a stretch get the chance to stage 7. You'll additionally see that you overcome the means quicker, as you figure out how to center. You may then extend your training by concentrating on a word or mantra or the like. Anything you find helpful or inspirational is an extraordinary mantra to utilize. Rehash the mantra quietly in your mind for the term of your training.

The hardest piece of reflection is staying with it. Numerous individuals get disheartened in light of the fact that they believe they "can't do it." To those inclination debilitated, let go of your desires. Without those desires, nobody is making a decision about your reflection. It is just for yourself and your own advantage. In the event that you stick to it for barely any months, you will arrive, ensured.

CHAPTER ONE:
HOW MEDITATION WORKS

There are a few distinctive contemplation systems that an individual can rehearse. The significant thing is to discover a contemplation strategy that you are OK with and attempt to stay with that one. On the off chance that you will in general bob around from one reflection system to the next you won't get the full advantages of contemplation. Contemplation has numerous advantages both physically, mentally and profoundly. A portion of these incorporates lower circulatory strain, improved skin tone, glad outlook on life, less pressure and only an overall sentiment of prosperity. Today we are simply going to give a concise blueprint of five of the significant reflection procedures.

Trataka

The main reflection system we need to discuss is Trataka Meditation. Trataka in Sanskrit intends to look or look. When performing Trataka Meditation an individual fixes their look on an outer article. This can be a speck on the divider, light fire or whatever. Trataka Meditation is an old yoga rehearsed to create focus and the Ajna (third eye) chakra. Fundamentally the individual looks at the article till the eyes start to water. As they are looking they let all contemplations course through their psyche and pass away. When the eyes start to water the eyes are then shut. When Trataka Meditation is performed with a light after the eyes start to water and are shut the individual focuses on the picture of the fire. From the outset, this will be an after picture, however, it will blur into seeing the picture with the psyches eye. This is a decent method to build up the third eye chakra.

Mantra

The following contemplation procedure is Mantra Meditation. Mantra Meditation is the place you state a word, for example, ohm again and again in your brain. In Mantra Meditation the word demonstrations like a vehicle that takes you to a condition of no idea. When rehashing the mantra or word it is extremely basic for the brain to float off into different musings.

At the point when this happens, the individual needs to delicate take their considerations back to the mantra and start rehashing it once. In Mantra Meditation the word that is rehashed is explicit to change the individual in a profound manner. Regularly a mantra will be given to a meditator by a master.

Chakra

The third contemplation method is Chakra Meditation. There are seven significant chakras in the human body. When performing Chakra Meditation the individual will concentrate on a particular chakra to scrub or empowering that chakra. Chakra Meditation can renew a person's body through the purifying, reviving procedure. As the chakras are interrelated it is encouraged to begin with the root chakra and stir your way up when performing Chakra Meditation. While doing Chakra Meditation you can likewise utilize the guide of gems to help in the purging, rejuvenation process. Chakra Meditation can be an incredible contemplation for recuperating and the clearing of negative feelings.

Vipassana

The forward reflection method is Vipassana Meditation. Vipassana Meditation is perhaps the most established type of contemplation and is utilized to pick up understanding into one's nature and the idea of the real world. The objective of Vipassana Meditation is to finish languishing over the person. This is cultivated by wiping out the three conditions which are fleetingness, enduring and not-self. Subsequent to rehearsing Vipassana Meditation for a significant stretch the meditator should go to a point where they separate these three conditions from themselves and accomplishing a nirvana. It is accepted that all physical and mental conditions are not part of the genuine self or the "I" and ought to be killed with the act of Vipassana Meditation.

Raja

The last contemplation system we will discuss is Raja Meditation. In Raja Meditation the brain is viewed as lord and it is the psyches' occupation to tame the feelings and the body. Raja Meditation endeavors to have the brain bring the body and feelings under unlimited oversight. Raja Meditation and related practices is a very order sort of reflection.

At the point when an individual takes up Raja Meditation, they are relied upon to surrender things like sex, liquor, meat and give close consideration to their activities. The thought in Raja Meditation for surrendering these things is it readies the body and brain for contemplation.

Above is a brief outline of five well-known contemplation procedures. I trust that this little article has given you enough data to point you toward the reflection system you might want to investigate more. It is proposed that in the event that you do take up a specific contemplation strategy that you follow a decent nitty-gritty program.

As you will find there are bunches of ways to deal with contemplation; several distinct tips and procedures. These all work; surely initially they help to center your focus. It is, be that as it may, significant not to get joined to a specific strategy or item. Regardless of anything else, contemplation is about a post acknowledgment that you have found the mystery hole that is as Wu portrays; nothingness, void, nonexistence. At exactly that point are you ruminating, and the key isn't to get a handle on what you have found in any case, essentially enable it to be, converging with the stillness, the quietness and the serenity that is the unadulterated substance of our universe.

It is the way to all ponder and the door to the pith of everything. It must be found inside, by converging with the quietness, the stillness and the serenity of the present minute. It is finding reflection and the mystery hole that prompts an existence of satisfaction, bliss, and all-out inward harmony. Life gets streaming, easy, and excellent and simultaneously you accomplish mindfulness which brings clearness, imagination and a profound feeling of the genuine reason that is essentially simply being.

Contemplation existed before history was recorded. Archeologists discovered old Indian sacred texts which definite the act of contemplation going back a huge number of years. It is an all-around archived practice of numerous world religions to incorporate Buddhism, Christianity, Hinduism, Islam, Jainism, Judaism, Sikhism, and Taoism. Spreading from the East reflection methods are presently rehearsed all through the world by a large number of individuals every day. Contemplation in Sanskrit is Dhyäna and is one of the eight appendages of yoga which prompts a territory of Samädhi (euphoria, ecstasy or harmony). The physical act of yoga, through the road of the breath, is in itself a moving contemplation which again is rehearsed by a huge number of individuals all through the world.

What are the different advantages of contemplation?

Studies have indicated that contemplation diminishes the negative impacts of pressure, tension, and despondency. By and large, we become more settled, more joyful and progressively satisfied.

Contemplation improves fixation, which is basic to understanding our actual potential. Centered fixation creates extraordinary force and when our forces of focus are improved we can utilize this to ruminate as well as in our different exercises as well. Some portion of accomplishing our objectives and wants is being able to ace our musings. By quieting the brain and centering our focus, we can encounter this self dominance and we can start to change and supplant our negative or undesirable considerations with positive ones. This move-in our manner of thinking adjusts our vitality to that of general vitality vibrations and we will start to see positive changes and enhancements all through all aspects of our lives.

Physically contemplation decreases pressure-related manifestations, for example, heart palpitations, strain and headache migraines, upset rest and bad dreams and depression. As stress and tensions are diminished we are really diminishing the likelihood of encountering any heart-related ailments.

Studies have additionally indicated that contemplation can soothe incessant agony, drop cholesterol levels and improve the circulatory strain. The progression of air to the lungs increments and improves and we will encounter a general more noteworthy feeling of prosperity.

How would I Meditate?

Buddhism frequently portrays contemplation as a method for 'preparing the frantic monkey', alluding to the brain as a distraught monkey, which is continually bouncing and dashing starting with one idea then onto the next. During a normal day, we think around 64,000 musings!

The Buddha said by the nonappearance of getting a handle on one is liberated. Contemplation isn't something you accomplish by attempting. Despite the fact that when you start to rehearse you are looking to reflect successfully, the more you attempt the more it will evade you. Reflection can be compared to holding a wet bar of cleanser; brief you are grasping it and the following it's gotten past you.

Reflection is tied in with giving up and to find the mystery hole you need to let everything go. Relinquish any result before you start.

There are numerous contemplation procedures, and more than a great many year's diverse reflection rehearses have advanced. The genuine embodiment of reflection, notwithstanding, is simply to sit and be. Simply you are going past the 'adapted' personality and lifting your psyche to a condition of unadulterated mindfulness.

While you can concentrate on an article or on your breath to assist you with reaching this state, at last, it is a characteristic procedure which advances after some time, the quintessence ought to consistently be in associating yourself with your source. You are searching internally without really endeavoring to do anything other than to simply sit and be.

It is additionally compelling to reflect on specific battles or issues we are encountering in our lives. For example, on the off chance that we need to go to a choice on a specific part of our life; a lifelong course, for instance, ruminating over this can assist us with arriving at the appropriate response. On occasion, the appropriate responses we are looking for can come into our brains very quickly. The intensity of centering fixation and coordinating that concentration towards a specific inquiry or subject can deliver stunning outcomes.

It is a smart thought to have a contemplation space. This can be a room or part of your home where you feel generally great. You may have delicate lighting, candles, incense, pads, blooms, and different items that summon sentiments of quiet and unwinding.

I intend to ruminate two times every day. Dawn and dusk are the best occasions of day for contemplation on the grounds that our brains are progressively open on these occasions. Dawn is the beginning of another day and wherever he hushes up, quiet and tranquil.

The day has not yet started and following a relaxing rest, our psyches will, in general, be quieter. At nightfall, the day is completion and contemplation as of now empowers us a calm reflection on the day we have recently passed. Our psyches are slowing down as of now before dozing, and the stillness and quiet that contemplation carries will be with us as we float off to rest, helping us to feel revived and stimulated when we stir the next morning.

Spot a pad on the floor and seat yourself with the goal that your base is half on and half off the pad. This will raise your hips and normally lift your spine and you will feel greater than if you were simply sitting on the floor. Bring yourself into a folded legs position. Customarily the lotus or half-lotus present is utilized when thinking yet in the event that you are not ready to easily sit in these postures, sit as is directly for you. Leave your spine alone upstanding and tilt your head with the goal that your eyes, when open, are fixed three feet before you. Spot your hands any place they feel good; one over the other in your lap, in a mudra with the tip of the thumb contacting the tip of the first or center finger to shape a circle, or basically place them on your thighs. Anything that is agreeable and feels directly for you.

As recently referenced there are numerous things you can concentrate on during contemplation; statues, blossoms or a solitary rose, silk scarves, candles, precious stones, music, mantras, and the breath to give some examples. Test yourself with each of these and find what works best for you.

As anyone might expect I have seen the easiest techniques as the best; the breath and a mantra. The model I have utilized all through the greater part of this area is the breath, which is by a long shot the most widespread focal point of reflection.

Close your eyes and start to concentrate on your breath. Concentrate on each breathes in and breathe out. Quietly saying the words 'SO' on the breath in and 'Murmur' on the breath out additionally help center. Enable your considerations to travel every which way however consistently return your concentration to your breath. In the event that you have picked an article, you would essentially concentrate on that item enabling the musings to travel every which way restoring your concentration to the item. After some time reflection gets simpler and you will discover as your self-authority develops you are effectively ready to sit for 20-30 minutes.

In any case, simply take a shot at accomplishing 5 minutes two times every day and afterward increment to 10, etc. Reflection can be compelling whenever. In the event that you are not ready to ruminate consistently locate some peaceful time when you can to enable yourself to just sit and be. Concentrate on your breath and imagine yourself sitting in someplace which will help realize a without a care in the world perspective. One of my top picks is on a seashore before a lovely quiet blue ocean. Pick something which feels right and valid for you. Be tolerant and delicate with yourself. As your capacity to contemplate expands, your degree of mindfulness develops. You will start to see enhancements with every day's reflection practice.

Enable yourself to turn into your own quiet eyewitness and essentially watch the breath. As you follow each breathe in and breathe out, contemplations will turn out to be slower. Allow the considerations to come and release them, just watching them and not getting connected to them. Your center is the breath, consistently come back to the cadenced breathe in and breathe out. At that point enable yourself to turn into the breath. With this blending comes to discharge and without a genuine fleeting acknowledgment, you are drenched in stillness, in the quiet and you have found the mystery hole. This is the spot of being, of the essence and of your actual self. Here you are at one with all the fixings; regardless of whether that be God, universe, Tao, divine awareness or whatever your term for it is, you are it, it is you and it and you are everything.

Would I Be Able To Show Myself; Do I Need An Instructor?

Contemplation is a voyage of self-revelation prompting self-authority that you can begin at this moment - today. There is nothing you have to discover that you don't have directly as of now inside you. Just sit and enable yourself to be. It is difficult, preparing the distraught monkey mind that races to start with one idea then onto the next in any case, with training, it turns into an inviting chance to invest energy with yourself.

A reflection educator can help and guide you through the act of contemplation and going to a gathering reflection session will empower you to impart the experience to other people, which can support your own training. Nonetheless, I would encourage you to begin rehearsing yourself as I have depicted in this area.

There is nothing a contemplation instructor can disclose to you that you don't as of now have any acquaintance with, you simply need to sit and be with yourself to find it.

Quiet isn't something we regularly experience consistently or even greeting so far as that is concerned. A great many people think that its extremely hard to truly unwind and give up, especially of their contemplations. The significant point to recall is that you are doing whatever it takes not to push your musings away, yet basically enabling them to be, without connection to them. This training after some time decreases the number of considerations, and interruptions, you experience during contemplation. Numerous individuals' lives are occupied and chaotic with work responsibilities, monetary weights, parenthood, mingling, leisure activities, interests and an entire rundown of different exercises that take up most within recent memory.

Settle on a cognizant choice to make time to ruminate. Focus on setting out without anyone else adventure of self-disclosure. Open your own incredible inventive potential which, with proceeded with the training of reflection, will be unbounded.

Long haul Lifestyle Changes to Help You Stay Calm

So as to turn into a progressively tranquil, quiet and serene individual over the long haul, it's significant that you make some long haul way of life changes that will furnish you with the capacity to all the more promptly control your passionate reactions. In any case, it's not just about the way of life, it's likewise about the mentality you bring into each snapshot of your life. Truth be told, both way of life and attitude go inseparably and cooperate to assist you with remaining quiet under tension.

Here are a few proposals to assist you with remaining quiet under tension as long as possible:

Get Good Quality Sleep and Exercise

Great quality rest and exercise are completely principal. Getting great quality rest will assist you with turning out to be substantially more sincerely strong.

Moreover, customary exercise will give you the vitality you have to deliberately and physically work through challenges unquestionably more adequately.

At the point when you're very much refreshed and when your body is feeling fit, you will normally have an additionally quieting vitality about you. It will be a lot simpler for you to remain loose during unsure occasions and troublesome minutes. You will end up feeling progressively focused, centered and in charge. This will furnish you with the clearness of mind you have to work through intense subject matters unmistakably more effectively.

Eat a Well Balanced Diet

Proceeding onward from the last point, it's likewise essential to eat well. Eating an all-around adjusted and solid eating routine, keeping yourself hydrated with water for the duration of the day, and evading the propensity for enjoying addictions will assist you with managing your feelings, and your reactions to the occasions and conditions of your life unmistakably more successfully.

Specifically stay away from drugs, liquor, sugar and caffeine addictions. These addictions will bother you, making it exceptionally hard to remain quiet and focused for the duration of the day.

Invest Energy Simplifying Your Life

It's hard to remain quiet and focused when you're living in confused chaos. When there's an excessive amount of messiness, when you're continually attempting to discover things, when you have such a large number of duties and obligations — undeniably increasingly then you can deal with — that is when things become exceptionally untidy. This is an unmistakable sign that your life is unreasonably confusing. It's hard to discover tranquility from inside on the off chance that you live in a frenzied and complex world.

Submit yourself today to the way toward streamlining your life and condition. For example, set aside some effort to sort out yourself and your things. Make a point to discover a spot for everything, and put everything in its place.

Make certain to de-mess your condition, to wipe out all unnecessary things, or essentially pack them away out of the picture and therefore irrelevant.

It's likewise critical to abstain from carrying on with a distracted way of life. Having an excessive number of duties and obligations don't give you enough time for yourself and your own enthusiastic needs. What you need is space, and a clean uncluttered condition to enable you to loosen up, unwind, and quiet down. This is the kind of condition that will support snapshots of self-reflection that you can use to help improve your choices pushing ahead.

Physically Slow Down

Living at a rushed pace can work very well for certain individuals. Indeed, there are individuals who blossom with criticalness, while as yet keeping up a quiet and focused vitality. Be that as it may, this sort of way of life isn't for everybody since it can prompt elevated levels of pressure and uneasiness.

On the off chance that you commonly experience the ill effects of pressure and nervousness consistently, at that point it's a reasonable sign that you are living too hysterically. There's simply an excessive amount of going on in your life, and right now you're only incapable to deal with yourself or your conditions. In such occurrences, it's essential to start backing things off. This, obviously, isn't simple.

There's simply such a great amount to do this brief period. Be that as it may, what you should do is re-organize things so as to help make the reality you have to back off.

Backing off doesn't really imply that you do everything all the more gradually. It does, nonetheless, imply that you do things all the more deliberately. In this way as opposed to hurrying through an assignment, thoroughly consider the undertaking and set aside a little effort to think about how to best take a shot at this errand in the best and time-effective way.

Backing off likewise implies discovering time for times of unwinding. It implies taking customary idea breaks. Thought-breaks are times for the duration of the day when you take a few minutes to isolate yourself from your errands and exercises to simply plunk down and consider your choices and activities.

These snapshots of self-reflection could give you some intriguing experiences that will assist you with working significantly more beneficially pushing ahead.

Reliably Build Your Support Network

During snapshots of extraordinary passionate change, it's critical to have individuals whom you can converse with and connect with. These individuals are a piece of your encouraging group of people. They are there to help you during troublesome snapshots of your life, and you are likewise there to help them in their passionate and physical battles.

Take some time currently to consider the sort of individuals that could increase an incredible value. Additionally, consider the individuals you could promptly help and support. Scribble down the names of every one of these people and concede to routinely keeping in contact with them. You could even make a passionate Mastermind gathering. This is the place you welcome similar people to a party once every week or month where you examine issues, concerns, and other passionate battles.

Your encouraging group of people will give you a stay you can use during troublesome passionate snapshots of your life. They will ingrain inside you the smoothness you need when there are enthusiastic tempests preparing around you.

Plan for Difficulties in Advance

Probably the most ideal approaches to remain quiet, engaged and focused consistently, is to plan for apparently startling misfortunes, troubles, and issues ahead of time. Obviously, you may be feeling that on the off chance that something is unforeseen, at that point there's definitely no real way to plan for it. In this way how about we take a gander at it another way:

Taking time to consider and planning for conceivable future situations brings them from the domain of the "obscure" into your cognizant mindfulness. In this way, what was surprising previously, is presently something you are prepared to handle at the time or later on.

At the point when you have a full and finish consciousness of what you will do in the following minute when things change, you will normally be increasingly quiet, gathered and genuinely focused.

It's frequently those startling minutes when occasions and conditions get you off guard lead to passionate change and overpower. In any case, given the way that you are currently arranged for the potential outcomes, you will, in this manner, be in a significantly more great situation to remain quiet and gathered during these troublesome snapshots of your life.

Thoroughly consider Your Decisions in Advance

Proceeding onward from the last point, it's additionally significant that you think about the outcomes of your decisions, choices, and activities ahead of time. It's entirely conceivable that specific choices can lead you down one way, and different choices will lead you down a totally unique way. Both of these ways have results and certain results that you should remember. A portion of these results may lead you into a passionate tornado, while different results may be somewhat more positive.

Thinking about the short and long haul conceivable outcomes of your decisions and choices will place you in the driver's seat of your life. Your mind will be arranged and prepared to manage various situations and circumstances. What's more, when your brain is readied, your feelings will be relentless and you will react proactively to the occasions and conditions of your life. This will leave you feeling quieter and focused pushing ahead.

Perhaps the most ideal approaches to recognize the potential results of your decisions and choices is to just set aside some effort to sit and reflect in a calm spot. Simply sit, and envision "in the event that I settle on this decision at the present time, it will in all probability result in... ". Set aside an effort to think about every one of the conceivable outcomes, and afterward set yourself up intellectually and physically for all the potential results.

While overseeing wretchedness the standard game plan in endeavoring to overcome the signs and symptoms of tendency disheartened is by visiting your PCP, restorative administration master or expert, whereby the shot of a psychotropic prescription or two is embraced to "help" you adjust. Regardless, does this genuinely manage the issue of overcoming despairing?

Or then again does it basically cover the issue with an invention coat?

There is a lot of discussion over the "compound lopsidedness in the cerebrum" speculation, as a result of the route that there is no proof to support this and no authentic tests are ever finished by an authority or advisor to develop if in truth the disheartened individual has an "engineered inconsistency".

What a pro can and should do in the essential event, if treating a patient who is debilitated or encountering wretchedness, is to do a cautious physical enrollment of the body to choose whether there are any organ breakdowns or issues similarly as whatever other physical issues that could be causing the disheartened state. There should in like manner be an enrollment to check whether the body is encountering a supplement or mineral need, and accepting this is the situation, normal improvements should be prescribed to alter that deficiency.

Take a Stroll to Help with Depression

This may seem, by all accounts, to be distorted in see yet taking a walk can help decrease the reactions of misery or uneasiness, and can have especially therapeutic results.

Someone who is disheartened or feeling anxious has, to some degree, their thought stuck or concentrated where it counts on themselves or on a particular difficulty or disaster, paying little mind to whether it is known or not, that is causing the debilitated tendency. For example, in case one had startlingly lost a companion or relative or a livelihood, by then fairly this causes stagger and excited torment. It can moreover be the circumstance that someone you are related to is continually tormenting or undermining you, which makes you pensive individual and feel terrible about yourself and lose courage.

These adversities, dazes, and inconveniences cause one to concentrate on the horrendous experiences which, over some indistinct time allotment, can make one feel low or disheartened. Thusly, the inspiration driving taking a walk is to an outgoing person your thought by putting your thought onto nature around you and expelling it from the shock, anguish or awful experiences.

Directly it's not just an example of going out and taking a ten-minute walk, you should go out and purposely look at things; you should look at and watch the things, houses, people, animals, the things around you.

You should see the black-top before your feet, you should look at the divider and the squares and the weeds getting out of them, you should look at the individual walking near you, etc.

This is an authentic practical exercise and if you continue looking, look, look, you will, at last, up giving more thought to nature and less thought will be revolved around your issues or melancholy. It is difficult for someone to deal with their issues effectively in case they are stuck in a pit of a disheartened state.

So with this task of taking a walk and looking, it ought to be continued until YOU see some improvement. It will be seen after some time doing this movement, a qualification in mien, or viewpoint of the earth, or essentially some degree of mitigation. This is a substantial explanation to stop. Make an effort not to go past this substantial articulation and don't stop the action until YOU see a positive change.

There is no set time designation in doing this action as each individual responds in a sudden manner. It should be done as long as major for each individual and should be done routinely.

CHAPTER TWO:
THE IMPORTANCE OF A
RIGHT WAY TO BREATHE

Breathing is the principal thing we do when we are conceived and the exact opposite thing we do before we kick the bucket yet what amount of significance do we provide for relaxing?

We can remain alive for extensive stretches without eating, drinking or dozing, however in the event that we can not inhale, we kick the bucket inside a couple of moments.

Shockingly, a large portion of us doesn't mull over our example of breathing… since it's programmed and we as a whole do it all things considered 20,000 times each day, however, why breathing appropriately is so significant?

Breathing is significant for two reasons:

1. it supplies our bodies and its different organs with oxygen, which is fundamental for our endurance.

Actually, through our breathing, we give oxygen to our body which can not be put away and must be renewed consistently and relentlessly, so it is essential to realize how to inhale appropriately.

Likewise, the oxygen enables the mind to work and if the oxygen is rare the blood must stream quicker.

2. With our breathing, we likewise dispose of waste items and poisons from the body.

Through our breathing, we carry oxygen to our body as well as discharge lethal substances that we have made and with terrible breathing these can without much of a stretch stagnate in our bodies and harm our indispensable capacities.

Shockingly, the vast majority of us utilize just 33% of the real breathing limit and, in this manner, we can not inhale well.

A few indications of a terrible relaxing:

- ❖ Hold our breath now and again
- ❖ Feel the requirement for a long breath
- ❖ Have a short breath
- ❖ Ran exhausted when we are moving quicker.

Our breathing is likewise the connection between our body and our psyche and for both to work well, they need oxygen.

On the off chance that our method for breathing is short and speedy our brains will be apprehensive and fomented.

On the off chance that our breathing is unpredictable the brain is on edge and upset.

One of the primary drivers of terrible breathing can be an absence of activity, yet it isn't generally so.

By figuring out how to inhale well we will get more beneficial and more grounded, yet not just:

Realizing how to inhale likewise helps us to control our feelings (outrage included) and fears and keep a reasonable and sharp personality.

On the off chance that our breathing is profound, slow and customary then our mind will arrive at a condition of serenity and quiet.

At the point when we are vexed or focused on our breathing turns out to be snappy and shallow. Breathing profoundly and gradually in a split second quiets us down intellectually just as physically.

Focusing on our breathing, additionally causes us to live the present and feel invigorated.

All the time our psyche is contemplating something while our body is accomplishing something different, accordingly, our brain and our body are not bound together.

With breathing activities, breathing in and breathing out, we carry our brain and body to cooperate in light of the fact that both are centered around something very similar and as I referenced in my last post we can feel invigorated in light of the fact that we are embracing current circumstances.

We can figure out how to inhale appropriately by rehearsing some breathing activities.

Breathing Exercises:

How about we start with a straightforward breathing activity that should be possible whenever of the day, in three basic developments, in any event for two or three minutes:

1) Do a profound inward breath

2) Hold your breath for a couple of moments

3) Then do a profound exhalation

On the off chance that you feel a slight feeling of vertigo, don't stress, it is because of the flood of a more prominent volume of oxygen to the mind.

I recommend to rehash this activity a few times for the duration of the day, particularly now and again when we are feeling especially unsettled, our resolve is low or in any event, when we feel tired.

❖ Complete Breathing

Step by step instructions to do it:

1) Stand up with your arms outstretched at your sides. At that point breathe out through our nose, discharging our lungs totally.

2) Inhale gradually through our nose and as we breathe in we have to push out the belly first and afterward the chest.

3) While we are as yet breathing in gradually we bring our arms over our head and pull up on

our toes and need check to 10 to finish these developments.

At the point when we get the opportunity totally to 10, we join the palms of our hands together over our head and hold it in this situation for a couple of seconds.

4) Exhale gradually through our nose tallying to 10 and simultaneously gradually we bring down our arms and spot our feet on the ground.

Rehash the activity three to multiple times, immediately.

The activity can likewise be performed from a sitting or lying position, without arm developments.

❖ Exercise lying in a prostrate situation, in a level situation, with our back on the ground.

We start to inhale uniformly and tenderly concentrating on the development of our stomach.

As we inhale we let our stomach ascend so as to carry air into the lower some portion of our lungs and as our lungs load up with air, our chest starts to rise while bringing down our stomach. During this activity, we should not endeavor.

The length of the exhalation will be longer than the motivations.

We can rehash the activity multiple times.

It isn't classified "The Breath of Life" to no end. One of the most essential elements of the human body, breathing not just energizes the body with oxygen, it can likewise clear a foggy personality and help reinforce the muscles. However, hardly any individuals figure out how to take in a manner that enables the body to work the manner in which it should.

The Process of Breathing

Before you can comprehend appropriate breathing procedures, it is imperative to know a little about how your body relaxes. At the point when you take in or breathe in, the muscle on the base of your ribcage, called your stomach, agreements, and moves to descend. This enables the lungs to have abundant space to grow. The muscles between your ribs, called the intercostal muscles, agreement to pull your ribcage upward and outward. As your lungs grow, the air is sucked in through your nose and mouth and goes down your trachea to your lungs. In the wake of going through your bronchial cylinders, the air, at last, arrives at the air sacs where oxygen is passed into the circulatory system. Simultaneously, the carbon dioxide goes into the air sacs from the circulation system and is ousted from the body as you breathe out. Overall, this procedure is rehashed between 17,000-

30,000 per day, consistently, up to an individual is alive.

A Better Way to Breathe

Since they are such huge numbers of frameworks impacting everything with every single breath, it is imperative to enable these organizing procedures to work the way they should.

❖ This starts, as a matter of first importance, with extraordinary stance. Sitting upright enables the lungs to extend rapidly and effectively with each breath. In like manner, sitting upright encourages air to go into the lungs and carbon dioxide to go out of the lungs unobstructed. In the event that you are sitting at your work area and feel foggy or generally deadened, pause for a minute to reposition your body with a straight back to see a prompt improvement at how well oxygen is arriving at your circulation system and in this way your cerebrum.

❖ While numerous individuals center around totally breathing in so as to improve their breathing, the vast majority just breathe out 70 percent of the carbon dioxide in their lungs. Attempt, rather drive the entirety of the let some circulation into of your lungs just as you are blowing bubbles. Not exclusively will your body reward you with moment vitality, you will see the amount increasingly productive you are in filling your lungs.

The Breath/Health Connection

Each framework in the body depends on oxygen. From perception to processing, compelling breathing can not just furnish you with a more prominent feeling of mental lucidity, it can likewise assist you with resting better, digest nourishment all the more proficiently, improve your body's insusceptible reaction, and diminish feelings of anxiety. Numerous individuals who practice yoga, particularly the individuals who center around the act of Pranayama, or breath control, have been appeared to manage the thoughtful sensory system, or the piece of the body that controls breathing, pulse and circulatory strain.

The Significance Of Relaxing

The human body can endure 3 weeks without nourishment, 3 days without water, however just 3 minutes without air – except if you are one of those freaky free jumpers, which I'm accepting you are definitely not.

Without air the cerebrum keeps from oxygen, ordinary real capacities stop to exist and basically amazing. That makes breathing high on the need list for human life. In any case, for a large portion of us, we don't pressure or stress over-breathing, regardless of whether there will be sufficient air to inhale or even how we inhale until we have lung contamination or a disease of the lungs which breaking points or bargains our capacity to relax.

To put it plainly, we underestimate breathing and regularly don't give it particularly consideration.

Breathing is something the body does naturally. In any case, did you realize that the manner in which we inhale changes relying upon our perspective and how we feel? Have you seen how your breathing theme changes with your feelings or in specific circumstances? At the point when we are focused or dreadful, we will, in general, take quick and shallow breaths, while when we are loose and calm we inhale tenderly and all the more relentlessly.

On the off chance that we hold our breath or change the rate at which we take in and out, we can really change how we feel. The manner in which we inhale can be effectively constrained by basically focussing on the breath and how we are relaxing. For instance, when we inhale delicately we send a sign to the body that says I am loose and that all is sheltered and well. Accordingly, the body creates fewer pressure hormones and builds feel-great hormones (endorphins).

The Advantages Of Relaxing

The first and most significant advantage of breathing is that breath is life – without it, we wouldn't be alive. We can't live without the breath as it brings us oxygen.

In any case, did you ever think that the manner in which that we inhale could affect the body, more so than simply giving the body oxygen?

Believe it or not – how we inhale and the manner by which we inhale influences our body and how we feel, and it even modifies our pulse, circulatory strain, feelings of anxiety and our wellbeing.

Strikingly, this has been asserted in thinks about that have demonstrated that the manner in which we inhale influences our sensory system, hormone creation, battle flight reaction, feelings of anxiety, heartbeat and rate, circulatory strain and processing.

We inhale by and large from 1700 to 2100 times each day. That is a ton of in and out; air going through our nose and lungs and into our course and plenty of breathing muscles and chest dividers growing and contracting, rising and falling.

At the point when we experience issues breathing appropriately, we can create conditions like the brevity of breath, mouth breathing or rest disarranged breathing like rest apnoea where we really stifle for breath in our rest. Stress brought about by tension can likewise make it difficult for us to inhale appropriately.

Breathing through the nose channels the air and cleans it so it is prepared for use once it enters our lungs. At the point when we mouth inhale the unfiltered air can really hurt our body, prompting irritation which builds our hazard for constant wellbeing conditions like coronary illness.

On the off chance that we are gagging for air during rest, this additionally prevents us from dozing profoundly and prompts tiredness, weariness, and depletion and again expands our danger of unexpected weakness.

With breathing is so essential to life and the manner by which we inhale having such an effect on our wellbeing and prosperity, would it not be reasonable to turn out to be increasingly mindful of how we inhale in order to have the option to decide to take such that supports us to be progressively solid and feel more in charge of ourselves?

Picking how to relax

- ❖ Can we decide to take in a manner that enables us to feel more calm, less focused and in charge of life?
- ❖ Can we utilize our breath to feel progressively associated, be less receptive to circumstances, have less pressure and improve our wellbeing?

Indeed we can, it is as simple as relaxing... indeed, as simple as picking how to relax.

❖ As simple as breathing delicately in and out through your nose.

❖ As simple as watching and watching your breath as frequently as you can during the day.

❖ As simple as setting aside some effort to stop and take yourself back to breathing a delicate breath.

CHAPTER THREE:
BEING PRESENT TO THE MOMENT, FEEL THE SPACE AROUND YOU

Holding space is a cognizant demonstration of being available, open, permitting, and defensive of what other necessities in every minute. The term has been developing in prominence among guardians, healers, yogis, and profound searchers. It's an extensively utilized expression to characterize the demonstration of "being there" for another. The impacts of this training, nonetheless, go a lot further than just contribution support.

Think about the individual words for a minute. To hold intends to grasp or encompass a person or thing in your grip. Physically, this may appear as an embrace or the support of a submit yours. Be that as it may, you can likewise grasp somebody non-physically with your aim, consideration, and vitality. Space alludes to the prompt condition you are offering to another. This, as well, might be the physical space of a room, yet more as often as possible alludes to the psychological and passionate condition you are in with others. Set up together, these words exemplify the standard of encompassing the earth with your mindfulness in a way that gives solace and empathy to all.

Holding space includes a few explicit characteristics of deliberately identifying with others, the entirety of which are more prominent than the individual parts. How about we investigate these properties and perceive how they can extend your capacity to hold space for other people.

Security

A key segment to holding space is the nature of security. For others to be open, certified, and in many cases defenseless, they should have a sense of safety and have a feeling of trust. Individuals won't let down their barriers until they realize it is protected to do as such.

Like a medieval church building settled inside the city's fortification dividers, you have to make a situation wherein all who enter feel shielded from hurt.

This security infers an implicit "sheepdog" mindset that fills in as a watchman and genuinely looks after secrecy, straightforwardness, and perfection in all you state and do.

Suspended Self-Importance

A fundamentally significant part of holding space is the understanding that it's not about you. At the point when you hold space you should settle on the cognizant choice to jettison your self-image. Holding space is tied in with serving others and your own interests or needs are not part of the procedure. Suspending your feeling of pomposity can be testing and ought to be viewed as an essential for the training. In the event that you aren't ready to place your inner self in the back for a period, you'll be ill-suited to be available for the requirements of others. Holding space requires radical lowliness and the readiness to be a transitory overseer of the sentiments and worries of another.

Consideration

One of the most valuable endowments you can give another is the endowment of your full and finish consideration. Notwithstanding, listening mindfully without the need to react, interfere, or remark is an expertise that takes significant practice to ace. Indeed, even with the best of goals, your self-image may sneak back in; it searches for chances to unpretentiously make things about you rather than the other.

When holding space you should work tirelessly to keep in touch, be liberated from interruptions, be completely mindful, and develop a transparency or "space cognizance" in which there is no "me," yet rather the ever-present observer of the sounding leading body of awareness.

To this end, make the pledge to develop what British creator Stuart Wilde called quiet force by fighting the temptation to talk except if you are asked to. This, combined with your full mindfulness, can be a significantly incredible encounter for those in your quality. Your consideration, engaged and comprehensive of anything that is going on at the time, open the entryway for others to see the impression of their own spirit in you—the Self conversing with itself.

Practice Acceptance

Holding space is tied in with permitting—enabling this individual or gathering to feel what they feel. Enabling them to state what they have to state. Enabling yourself to be whatever they need you to be at the present time. Holding space, consequently, isn't tied in with controlling anything. Your job is that of a gatekeeper of the space. Like two measured hands loaded up with water, you are there to hold the other with your mindfulness. In doing as such, you should enable that experience to take whatever shape it will.

Acknowledge this minute for what it's worth. Acknowledge others as they seem to be, with no longing to transform them, or need them to be something other than what's expected. This, as well, can be a test since you are adapted to quickly attempt to change things you think ought to appear as something else. In any case, in holding space, rehearsing acknowledgment gives others an extremely valuable blessing—the opportunity to be similarly as they may be.

Nonjudgement

Holding space is an unbiased procedure. You're not there to condemn or to assess another. At the point when you judge another person's experience you make extra mental static that will just disrupt the general flow and darken reality. At the time when you're holding another's feelings of dread, enduring, or melancholy, your conclusions are insignificant.

Except if you've experienced what they're experiencing, you'll never genuinely comprehend their emotions. Being there is sufficient. Great and awful are simply a matter of viewpoint and at this time, your point of view isn't the one that is significant.

Sympathy

Despite the fact that you nonjudgmentally practice acknowledgment with your complete consideration, that doesn't mean you wouldn't favor things to be better. Empathy is a fundamental quality for the act of holding space. To grasp another in the acknowledgment is a demonstration of empathy all by itself. In your receptiveness, to the torment of others, you are basically saying, "How might I help you? I don't need you to hurt.

What would I be able to do to help bolster your most elevated great?" Even if not spoken so anyone might hear, these expectations to calm the enduring of others are the pith of sympathy.

As a rule, essentially being a caring nearness can realize a profound good feeling that facilitates the agony of another. The world can utilize more empathy, so the act of holding space gives a chance to persistently fabricate this essentially significant aptitude.

Seeing

Seeing enables you to have an extraordinary influence while holding space—that of the onlooker. Like in quantum material science, the spectator is the thing that triggers the breakdown of the flood of potential into a molecule, the non-neighborhood into the limited wonder. However, this doesn't include any activity on the onlooker's part. In holding space you're only there as the observer, practically like a fly on the divider. Normally, you can take an interest whenever mentioned to do as such, however, basically, your job is that of the watcher.

It is said that when Gautama (the future Buddha) was very nearly illumination, he was enticed by the powers of murkiness and their lord, the devil Mara. With his whole devil armed force diving upon them, Mara requests the Gautama produce an observer to his enlivening. Gautama just contacts the earth with his fingers and says, "The earth itself is my observer."

With this motion, Mara and his arm disappear, and Gautama turns into the Buddha or Awakened One. Like the earth the Buddha contacts, you are the observers to the individuals who you hold space for.

Through the act of holding space, you fill in as a compartment for which the mending and change can occur. It's an incredible endowment of essence that you can provide for others through the nature of your consideration.

Moreover, a large number of us experience difficulty unwinding in light of the fact that we have no clue how to associate with the experience that is unfurling at the present time. It's practically new on the grounds that we are so used to speculation, thinking, contemplating everything, Now is continually happening.

It's going on right now. The distinction for us is in what it feels like to be available. Certain careful practices help get us closer to the present time and place where the future and the past can't be found.

❖ Do less. Being in the "now" minute resembles glancing through a focal point. On the off chance that the focal point is packed by recollections and future, it's so little you can't see through. Give up. Try not to attempt to try and be available. We can't make more space to encounter now and transparent the focal point by adding more to the image. This minute won't be something besides it is and we can't control it in any case. So simply stop. Quit everything. An astute instructor once stated, "nothing endures, in any event, for a moment." There is a component of giving up to be available, in light of the fact that we abandon attempting to get things going out and out — quit attempting to unwind, quit attempting to be open, quit attempting to be engaged, story attempting to complete everything. Things are continually moving and we can't feel it since we too caught up with being in charge constantly. Imagine a scenario where truly surrendered to attempting to do everything. We let go of the wheel, surrender control... and sink down inside with the breath. What's truly managing everything? What's underneath the surface? How do our feelings impact our capacity to be available?

❖ Inhale. At that point Exhale. A breath brings you here right away. Breath encourages us to let in the present experience we're having. A cycle of just breathing in, then breathing out is an incredible move out of the consistent agitating of the psyche. The brain can't complete 2 things on the double, similar to think and relax. So a breath dials into an alternate recurrence the NOW channel. You can tune into what your body is feeling. Feeling occurs in the body is a magnificent method to discover what the present minute is. Since the present minute offers no ensures that it will feel better, we may discover strain in the back, and some feelings sitting in the chest or stomach. We center around the sentiment of breathing, and abruptly our contemplations have been given up. Presently, we can take advantage of anything that is occurring without making a story. All of a sudden there's space to acknowledge being here right now in the entirety of its completion of feeling and feeling.

❖ Trust. This is the hardest one for me. Getting into the present minute is a certain something, and remaining there is a very surprising thing. It resembles not completely going into the room.

We get to the limit and look in, yet to enter completely into the new space of our present experience takes boldness and empathy. Feeling, we surrender control and let what needs to occur, occur. For a significant number of us, we ordinarily do the inverse. How are we expected to work while passionate? Well, how is it attempting to be occupied with our psychological motion pictures and constant examples that keep us stuck? Where is the satisfaction and wealth of life in stress and detachment? So: attempt trust. We've had the option to have a go at breathing and giving up, presently continue doing it. Bouncing go into constant reasoning and dependence on telephones will continue bothering us to quit breathing when you question and get eager. Oppose it. Remain profound, and let what's going on to come through — particularly the obstruction. It's a sense of self keeping you little and stuck. Traverse it. You can do this by put shortly alone to feel everything, completely. And afterward: open sky. Lighter chest.Opportunity. Trust the procedure. It's been around through the Buddhist posse for a long time on purpose.

Doing this at work is particularly useful when you discover the pressure has developed around you. Rehearsing these once as well as after some time enables our psyches to settle. Neighborhood classes are offered in many spots. Converse with companions about it, and go to a free class. Quest online for instructing and reflection gatherings. Purchase a book and attempt it at home. Do it in your work area. Do it when you're trapped in rush hour gridlock. Do it before shouting at your children in the market. The key is: simply practice. Being available is a lot simpler when you realize how to arrive.

CHAPTER FOUR: BEST MEDITATION TECHNIQUES

Contemplation is a transformational technique that causes us to unwind as well as improves our general prosperity. In case you're simply starting to ruminate or you've been needing to learn, there is an assortment of straightforward contemplation procedures you could begin with. Figuring out how to contemplate may appear to be an overwhelming errand for tenderfoots, however, the essentials are in reality quite direct. To find out about reflection procedures for amateurs, follow our guided contemplations for learners through the Mindworks App.

Fledglings Manual For Contemplation

The expression "contemplation" signifies various things to various individuals. There's otherworldly contemplation, unwinding reflection, reciting reflection, and a lot of others. Here at Mindworks we center around two standard sorts of contemplation: care and mindfulness reflection. With care, we train in completely possessing the present minute. By settling carefully in the present time and place, we can relinquish everything else that is engrossing us for a couple of moments, and this can be brilliantly unwinding. This is one motivation behind why care has been utilized so adequately to battle worry, for instance. What's more, how would we settle in the present time and place? A standout amongst other realized techniques urges us to sit carefully and just focus on the breath.

Mindfulness reflection utilizes the solidness picked up from care to investigate the mechanics of the brain –

recognition, feelings, sensations, etc. It's a further developed practice that prompts extraordinary experiences, and care is its premise.

In case you're simply starting, it's ideal to go slowly – on the off chance that you can ponder "strictly" for 5 or 10 minutes consistently that is an incredible beginning. As you get into the training, you can sit for longer periods, or you can take progressively visit "careful breaks" during your day on the off chance that you decide to. You'll before long find that you can't envision a day without contemplation.

Here are a few hints on the best way to do contemplation for learners:

1) Get agreeable

Locate a tranquil, quiet spot to rehearse your day by day contemplation. Next, pick a contemplation act that suits you. See our Take Your Seat video underneath for pointers. You can sit on a seat, pad or seat, however, attempt to sit upright – give specific consideration to your back. Keep up the arrangement without being too inflexible about it. Unwind!

2) Be present

When you've discovered your stance, check in with how your body feels – are there strains? In the event that there are, you can either watch them or welcome them to extricate up, tenderly. Shouldn't something be said about the eyes? While a few customs urge meditators to rehearse with their eyes shut, we suggest preparing to keep them half-open with your look coordinated down and before you. Having the eyes open assists with sharpness. Another bit of leeway is that as reflection turns into a standard practice, there won't be such a particular distinction between care on the pad and care in your day by day life.

Focus on what you hear, the sensations moving through your body, how it feels to stay there, what musings are meandering through your brain. Be available without making a decision about your experience.

3)   Focus on your breathing procedure

Your breathing should fall into place easily – don't constrain it. Try not to stress whether it is moderate, profound or reliable. After some time, as your mind quiets down, so does the breath. Set aside the effort to watch your breath, seeing the quality and beat of breath.

As you center around your breathing, your mind will presumably begin meandering. This is flawlessly ordinary, and it's extraordinary that you've gotten mindful of it. When you notice that your psyche has meandered, let the contemplations pass and delicately take your consideration back to the object of your reflection: your breath.

4) Feel the sensations streaming however the body

You can return to familiarity with your body in your reflection. This may incorporate a psychological body check. Start with your toes. How would they feel? Is there any strain? In case you're shoeless, would you be able to feel the development of the air on your toes, on your feet? In case you're wearing socks or shoes, attempt to decide the vibe of the texture or shoe material. Is there pressure? Delicateness? Is something nodding off? Try not to change or break down anything: simply notice. Step by step work your direction upwards, concentrating on every territory of the body, each part in turn. At the point when you discover your mind meandering, tenderly take your fixation back to your thought of your body. Following two or three minutes of this, you can restore your consideration regarding the breath or proceed with the body examination.

5) Practice makes great

Numerous experts, prepared meditators and amateurs the same, appreciate the "autopilot" feel of guided contemplation. There are numerous reflection assets out there, and a large portion of them are novice amicable. Obviously, we're inclined toward the Mindworks Meditation Courses, especially balanced Courses intended to motivate your everyday contemplation from beginning to end. You can without much of a stretch sign up and use it on your gadget.

Ordinary practice is the way to care contemplation. Taking 10 minutes of your day to think can do some incredible things over the long haul. In a little while, your day will feel deficient without it.

6) Make care a necessary piece of your way of life

Care is tied in with monitoring the present minute. It includes effectively preparing the brain to abide in the present time and place as opposed to go over past recollections or worry about what's to come. Although the present minute is all we've truly got, we seldom even consider it until we start ruminating. In any case, when we start, it resembles we've discovered the key that opens characteristics and experiences that have consistently been ready for whoever gets there first – we just never took the time or very knew how. Also, presently is all we have!

CHAPTER FIVE:
THE MOST EFFECTIVE METHOD TO START TO MEDITATE

It's amazingly hard for a novice to sit for a considerable length of time and consider nothing or have a "vacant personality." We have a few instruments, for example, an apprentice contemplation DVD or a cerebrum detecting headband to help you through this procedure when you are beginning. When all is said in done, the least demanding approach to start contemplating is by concentrating on the breath — a case of one of the most well-known ways to deal with reflection: fixation.

Focus Contemplation

Fixation contemplation includes concentrating on a solitary point. This could involve following the breath, rehashing a solitary word or mantra, gazing at a light fire, tuning in to a redundant gong, or checking dabs on a mala. Since centering the psyche is testing, a learner may contemplate for just a couple of moments and afterward work up to longer spans.

In this type of reflection, you essentially pull together your mindfulness on the picked object of consideration each time you notice your mind meandering. As opposed to seeking after arbitrary musings, you just let them go. Through this procedure, your capacity to think improves.

Care Contemplation

Care contemplation urges the expert to watch meandering considerations as they float through the psyche. The expectation isn't to engage with the musings or to pass judgment on them, yet just to know about each psychological note as it emerges.

Through care contemplation, you can perceive how your considerations and emotions will in general move specifically design.

After some time, you can turn out to be progressively mindful of the human propensity to rapidly pass judgment on an encounter as positive or negative, charming or horrendous. With training, an internal equalization creates.

In certain schools of contemplation, understudies practice a blend of fixation and care. Numerous orders call for stillness — to a more prominent or lesser degree, contingent upon the instructor.

Other Reflection Methods

There are different other reflection methods. For instance, everyday contemplation practice among Buddhist priests centers legitimately around the development of sympathy. This includes imagining negative occasions and recasting them in a positive light by changing them through sympathy. There are additionally moving contemplation strategies, for example, kendo, qigong, and strolling reflection.

Advantages Of Contemplation

In the event that unwinding isn't the objective of contemplation, it is regularly an outcome. During the 1970s, Herbert Benson, MD, a scientist at Harvard University Medical School, instituted the expression "unwinding reaction" subsequent to leading exploration on individuals who rehearsed supernatural reflection. The unwinding reaction, in Benson's words, is "an inverse, automatic reaction that causes a decrease in the movement of the thoughtful sensory system."

From that point forward, considers the unwinding reaction have reported the accompanying momentary advantages to the sensory system:

- ❖ Lower circulatory strain
- ❖ Improved blood dissemination
- ❖ Lower pulse
- ❖ Less sweat
- ❖ Slower respiratory rate
- ❖ Less nervousness
- ❖ Lower blood cortisol levels
- ❖ More sentiments of prosperity
- ❖ Less pressure
- ❖ Deeper unwinding

Contemporary specialists are currently investigating whether a predictable reflection practice yields long haul benefits, and taking note of constructive outcomes on the mind and resistant capacity among meditators. However, it merits rehashing that the motivation behind reflection isn't to accomplish benefits. To put it as an Eastern thinker may state, the objective of contemplation is no objective. It's just to be available.

In a Buddhist way of thinking, a definitive advantage of contemplation is freedom of the brain from connection to things it can't control, for example, outside conditions or solid interior feelings. The freed or "edified" professional never again unnecessarily follows wants or sticks to encounters, yet rather keeps up a quiet personality and feeling of inward concordance.

The most effective method to ponder: Simple contemplation for fledglings

This contemplation practice is a great prologue to reflection strategies.

1. Sit or lie serenely. You may even need to put resources into a contemplation seat or pad.
2. Close your eyes. We prescribe utilizing one of our Cooling Eye Masks or Restorative Eye Pillows if resting.

3. Make no push to control the breath; just inhale normally.

4. Focus your consideration on the breath and on how the body moves with every inward breath and exhalation. Notice the development of your body as you relax. Watch your chest, shoulders, rib confine, and gut. Basically concentrate on your breath without controlling its pace or force. In the event that your mind meanders, return your concentration back to your breath.

Keep up this reflection practice for a few minutes to begin, and afterward, attempt it for longer periods.

Contemplation is an extremely basic practice that individuals overcomplicate. This article centers around breathing contemplation, where you center around your breath. (Envision that!)

The essential thought of reflection is basic. Each time your mind starts to move its spotlight away from your breath and you lose all sense of direction in thought, you essentially take your consideration back to your breath. And afterward, you rehash this and again until your contemplation clock sounds. The fact of the matter is that each time you take your consideration back to your breath, you work out your "consideration muscle", in the event that you need to consider it that. At that point, after some time your center, fixation, and ability to focus improve, notwithstanding the plenty of different advantages referenced previously.

That is the fundamental thought of contemplation.

You will require two things to begin, yet you ought to have the two as of now.

You needn't bother with a lot to ponder, however you ought to have two things:

1. Something to sit on. There is such thing as standing contemplation and strolling reflection, however sitting reflection is the most widely recognized and the best spot to begin.

2. A clock. Since reflection is tied in with working out your "consideration muscle", checking a clock would to some degree nullify the point of contemplation since it would continually occupy your consideration away from your breath.

1. Something To Sit On

There are three choices for something to sit on during reflection.

A seat (decent in case you're beginning or have back issues)

Seats are extraordinary for in case you're simply beginning to reflect, or on the off chance that you have back issues and discover sitting on a contemplation pad awkward. In case you're new to contemplation, I prescribe utilizing a seat the initial barely any occasions as opposed to going out and purchasing a reflection pad. When you routinize reflection and become increasingly OK with it, at that point I would prescribe obtaining a contemplation pad; utilizing a seat from the outset will assist you with slipping your way into training.

A Contemplation Pad (Generally Normal)

A reflection pad (named a "zafu", envisioned right) is the most mainstream thing individuals sit on during contemplation. The extraordinary thing about a contemplation pad is it is most straightforward to sit in an upstanding position when you're on one, which improves your sharpness and the nature of your reflection (and subsequently, how gainful your sit is). With a seat or a contemplation seat, you might be enticed to droop, which can make you lose center.

A Reflection Seat (More Agreeable Than A Pad)

In case you're taller or discover a reflection pad excessively awkward, it merits giving a contemplation seat a shot. It will, in any case, drive you to sit upstanding, and you won't have the inclination to droop as much as you do on a seat.

Reflection seats additionally retain a great deal of the weight you would have generally applied to your legs, which makes contemplation considerably more agreeable.

Proposal

I prescribe that you sit on a seat the initial a few times you reflect, and afterward change to a contemplation pad (zafu) after you become increasingly alright with your training.

A reflection pad will keep you the most alarm during your contemplation, yet you likely don't make them lying around your home as of now. It additionally takes your body some time to adjust to sitting on one, which will make you sore when you first begin. In case you're generally fit and sound, however, I suggest utilizing a pad for the readiness it will give you.

In the event that you have leg issues, or are simply searching for something somewhat more agreeable than a reflection pad, I suggest utilizing a seat. In the event that you have back issues, I prescribe utilizing a seat – yet be cautious, on the grounds that however seats are progressively agreeable, it's simpler to lose center around one.

2. A clock

The second thing you'll require is a clock.

I suggest that you essentially utilize your telephone, however simply make a point to kill your telephone's radio before you start reflecting. Practically every telephone has a clock inherent, and on the off chance that you have a cell phone, odds are there is an extraordinary contemplation application for it as well.

❖ Insight Timer is a decent pick, and there's a free form of it accessible for iPhone and

Android. You can even observe who around the globe is contemplating when you are!

❖ If you're willing to make good a couple of bucks ($3.99), Meditate for iPhone is a decent pick, and it's the one I use. It's dead-basic and showcases a basic page of details after you finish.

Step By Step Instructions To Sit

❖ The greatest thing to recollect is to keep your back straight. Keep your back erect (in case you're in a seat it's best not to lay your back on the rear of the seat), and keep an upstanding stance. This keeps you alert and enables you to focus all the more effectively on your breath.

❖ Your eyes can be either shut or open. Once more, the objective of this entire "contemplation" thing is to work out your consideration muscle. On the off chance that you discover you can focus better on your breath with your eyes shut, the same number of individuals do, at that point, it's presumably best to keep them shut. In case you're worn out and wind up resting off when you close your eyes, take a stab at opening them somewhat and concentrating your look delicately on a space on the floor before you. For me, this becomes diverting, so I keep them shut and possibly open them in case I'm worn out.

❖ Don't stress over your hands. A few people like to frame hovers with their thumb and another finger, however, that doesn't generally make a difference, as I would see it. I normally simply rest my hands, palm down, on my legs, any place they feel the most agreeable.

❖ Cross your legs any way you need. I typically fold my legs before me, and I imagine that works fine for a great many people. On the off chance that you need to overlay your feet like a pretzel you can, however on the off chance that you use contemplation to fortify your consideration muscle, it might be least demanding to keep to a straightforward, leg over leg present.

❖ Look somewhat descending, regardless of whether your eyes are shut. This opens up your chest. Once more, however, discover a spot that is agreeable – one that keeps you upstanding and opens up your chest simultaneously.

❖ The greatest point I can make about how to sit is to discover a posture and stance that is both agreeable and keeps you upstanding. The rules above work best for me and the greater part of the individuals I know, however, they may not work for you. The most agreeable contemplation posture will give you so little sharpness that it will put you to rest, and the least agreeable posture will keep you alert, yet to the detriment of your solace.

The best exhortation I can offer is to attempt to discover a spot in the middle of that works the best for you.

What to do

The consideration you give the various things around you is a spotlight, and throughout the day you move it around and point it at various things, as a rule without pondering the way that you're doing this. As you move it around, you point it at all that you offer regard for in your life, from your cell phone to a discussion you're having, to a report you're composing. What's more, a great deal of the time, you direct it at more than each thing in turn. All things considered, more often than not you do.

CHAPTER SIX:
GETTING READY FOR
MEDITATION

Perhaps the best thing about contemplation, that training of discreetly watching your musings and emotions in your brain without judgment, is that you needn't bother with anything to rehearse. No contraptions or rigging are fundamental. You can rehearse contemplation on the tram. You can rehearse reflection in bed. You can rehearse reflection in the shower! Basically, take in and notice that you are taking in. At that point inhale out and notice that you are breathing out. That is it. You're thinking! There is no requirement for any arrangement or ceremony. Simply sit.

That being stated, on the off chance that you do have the opportunity, space, vitality, and want, you should set yourself up. Getting ready for reflection physically, intellectually, and profoundly can upgrade your thoughtful experience.

While thinking about contemplation readiness, it is basic to think about what style of reflection you intend to rehearse. Do you like to be guided through contemplation, during which time you tune in to somebody conversing with you smoothly? Would you like to rehearse purposefully concentrating on sympathy and graciousness while you ponder? Do you like to follow your breath and "simply be"?

Advantages of Meditation

There are numerous kinds of reflection. Whatever style you decide for your sitting, there are large numbers of advantages. Regardless of whether you decide to get ready for contemplation or only set aside some effort to purposefully inhale, it sure appears to merit checking out it! The aces of contemplation incorporate the accompanying:

- ❖ Anxiety alleviation
- ❖ Chronic help with discomfort
- ❖ Increased creative mind and inventiveness
- ❖ Increased mindfulness
- ❖ Stress the board

Planning for Meditation

On the off chance that reflection is valuable and you needn't bother with any hardware with which to rehearse, why it is useful to get ready for a contemplation sitting? Truth be told, there are a few physical, mental, and profound reasons why getting ready for reflection is a useful propensity. As you settle your body into an agreeable position, locate the best seating choice, and wear an inconspicuous dress, you help make clear vitality diverts in your body. At the point when your vitality channels are unblocked, the prana, or life power, can move through your framework effortlessly, making a general feeling of prosperity. As you get ready for reflection by setting an expectation, picking a physical point of convergence, or choosing a mantra, you set up for your psyche to concentrate on the present minute.

An investigation distributed in the Journal of Personality and Social Psychology showed that when you center around the present minute you improve mindfulness and increment constructive enthusiastic states. At long last, as you devote your reflective time to the opportunity and satisfaction of all creatures all over, including yourself, you make space to open to higher knowledge. Consolidating and regarding some comprehension of the interconnectedness all things considered (or any type of otherworldliness) into your life has been appeared to build strength, lower manifestations of melancholy, increment fulfillment with life, and increment future.

Anticipate the Unexpected

Every one of these arrangements expands the plausibility of a delightful contemplation experience. Similarly as with anything, notwithstanding, there are a few things for which you just can't get ready. At the point when you are pondering, any number of surprising sounds, musings, or sensations could occupy you from stillness. Actually, it is practically sure that something will divert you!

Despite the solace of your pad and the magnificence of your mantra, contemplations will sneak in. You will probably feel peculiar sensations or terrible feelings. You will probably get debilitated or redirected. Thus, set up all you need. Get ready as much as you possibly can, contingent upon your conditions. Yet in addition, just like the idea of the training, unwind and enable your reflective experience to just be what it will be.

Here are some useful hints to get ready physically, intellectually, and profoundly for reflection. I appreciate the recuperating advantages of this incredible practice.

Morning Meditation Tips

On the off chance that you ponder toward the beginning of the day, prepare to think by getting ready physically, intellectually, and profoundly. Morning reflection establishes the pace for your day. You can fuse goal setting, yoga asana practice, profound breathing systems, and journaling for an all-encompassing encounter—or essentially sit.

In the event that you don't have a great deal of time toward the beginning of the day rise, pee, reflect (RPM)! Get yourself up, utilize the bathroom, discover your pad, and sit. Reflection can be as basic or as perplexing as you make it. This act of meeting yourself as you are toward the beginning of the day can be a sweet and intriguing and exceptional inclination. It is profoundly helpful. Do it. On the off chance that you have additional time toward the beginning of the day, set aside some effort to set up your body, brain, and soul for a contemplation practice.

Physically:

- ❖ Wash your face to wake up.
- ❖ Brush your teeth to feel invigorated and clean after rest.
- ❖ Put on agreeable garments so you will be unperturbed while you sit.
- ❖ Clear any attire or mess from your reflection territory.
- ❖ Make your bed.
- ❖ Let the pooch out.
- ❖ Put your telephone on quiet or don't upset with the goal that you won't be disturbed.
- ❖ Go to the washroom.
- ❖ Find an agreeable seat on a pad or seat.
- ❖ Light a flame to emblematically welcome light into your space.
- ❖ Set up your clock or set up your guided reflection application.

❖ Take a couple of purifying breath spins in and out through your nose to quiet your sensory system before you start.

Intellectually:

❖ Set an aim or pick a mantra for your morning contemplation.
❖ Pull a prophet card or read an avowing entry in a book to move your day.
❖ Mentally focus on remaining situated and present in your contemplation for the span you settled on.

Profoundly:

❖ Dedicate your opportunity to your own self-care and mending.
❖ Send out a desire of prosperity, harmony, and love for somebody, a particular gathering of individuals, or all creatures.

Night Meditation Tips

On the off chance that you ponder at night, prepare to reflect physically, intellectually, and profoundly.

Night contemplation establishes the pace for rest. Similarly likewise with a morning reflection, with a night contemplation, you can consolidate expectation setting, yoga asana work on, breathing strategies, and journaling for a comprehensive encounter—or essentially sit.

In the event that you don't possess a ton of energy for contemplation rehearses at night, sit directly before bed. You could even protest bed. In the event that you figure you will nod off, sit on your bed against the divider as opposed to leaning back. Prepare yourself for rest and afterward ruminate for a brief period before you float off. This act of interfacing with yourself at night can be a pleasant method to check-in and wind as the day progressed. Investing significant time for individual reflection and inward concordance before bed is exceptionally helpful. Do it. In the event that you have additional time at night, set aside some effort to set up your body, brain, and soul for a contemplation practice.

Physically:

- ❖ Wash your face or shower to truly and emblematically discharge the day.
- ❖ Brush your teeth to feel invigorated and clean before rest.
- ❖ Put on agreeable garments or nightwear so you can creep directly into bed post-contemplation.
- ❖ Clear any dress or mess from the day's exercises from your reflection zone.
- ❖ Let the pooch out.
- ❖ Put your telephone on quiet or don't upset with the goal that you won't have interfered with. (Even better, turn your telephone right off and don't walk out on until after your morning contemplation!)
- ❖ Go to the washroom.

❖ Set up your bed for rest time: pull out your rest veil, put your diary or book on the bedside table, and move any enhancing pads aside.

❖ Light a flame to emblematically welcome light into your space.

❖ Dim the lights and enable your eyes to conform to the dull.

❖ Find an agreeable seat on a pad or seat.

❖ Set up your clock or set up your guided contemplation application.

❖ Take a couple of purifying breath spins in and out through your nose to quiet your sensory system before you start.

Intellectually:

❖ Write down or consider three individuals or occasions from your day that you are particularly appreciative of.

❖ Set a goal or pick a mantra for your night reflection.

❖ Pull a prophet card or read an asserting section in a book to move your reflection and your fantasies.

❖ Mentally focus on remaining situated and alert in your contemplation for the term you chose.

Profoundly:

❖ Dedicate your opportunity to your own self-care and mending.

❖ Send out a desire of prosperity, harmony, and love for somebody, a particular gathering of individuals, or all creatures.

Gathering Meditation

In the event that you ruminate in a gathering, get ready physically, intellectually, and profoundly. Gathering reflection keeps you liberated from specific interruptions you may experience while pondering your own. Gathering contemplation additionally mitigates the test of control required to reflect solo. Regardless of whether your gathering is a formal, guided assembling or just a gathering of companions sitting together, you can consolidate goal setting, yoga asana work on, breathing methods, and journaling for a comprehensive encounter—or essentially join the gathering and sit.

The act of thinking in a gathering is a significant component of the profound reflection way of life; Satsang, or communing with others and sharing information, brings the fulfillment of "being at home on the planet." Connecting with your own internal life while in the midst of a gathering of correspondingly engaged meditators has its advantages. Contemplating in a gathering can:

- ❖ Strengthen your associations.
- ❖ Allow you to help each other and keep each other responsible to your objectives.
- ❖ Help you gain from experienced meditators or gain from directing and showing new meditators.
- ❖ Help you remain spurred and focused on a standard practice

Consider joining the 21-Day Meditation Experience through the Chopra Center for an online gathering contemplation experience. Or then again search for a neighborhood in-person guided contemplation course or continuous class close to you. Or then again have your own gathering reflection! In the event that you have time before your gathering reflection practice, take a break to set up your body, brain, and soul for the sitting.

Physically:

- ❖ Wear agreeable garments.
- ❖ Wash off any solid aromas or scents so as not to be an undesirable interruption to the gathering.
- ❖ Put your telephone on quiet or don't upset with the goal that you won't intrude on the sitting.
- ❖ Go to the washroom.

❖ Mindfully welcome the educator/manager if there is one and offer grins or greetings with others in the gathering.

❖ Find an agreeable seat on a pad or seat.

❖ Take a couple of purging breath spins in and out through your nose to quiet your sensory system before the gathering contemplation starts.

Intellectually:

❖ Listen to a gathering goal or set a goal for the reflection.

❖ Prepare yourself for a portion of the difficulties of a gathering sitting: others can make diverting commotions, enter the space with odd aromas, or generally upset the vitality of the reflection space.

❖ Mentally focus on remaining situated and present in the contemplation for the span the gathering has settled on or that you will enable yourself to leave the space unobtrusively in the event that it turns out to be excessively overpowering.

Profoundly:

- ❖ Dedicate your opportunity to your very own self-care and mending.
- ❖ Send out a desire of prosperity, harmony, and love for somebody, a particular gathering of individuals, or all creatures.

While reflecting doesn't require any noteworthy measure of planning, setting yourself up to be agreeable and present physically, intellectually, and profoundly, can upgrade your contemplation practice. Regardless of whether you intend to sit in the first part of the day, night, solo, or in a gathering, purging your body, psyche, and soul before you sit can help make for a wonderful and mending contemplation. I appreciate the adventure!

CHAPTER SEVEN:
BEST MEDITATION
POSITIONS

Why position matters

Contemplation is picking up fame because of its endless advantages.

Reflection isn't one-size-fits-all — many varieties and methods are accessible to you. Be that as it may, you don't have perused each book on the subject or start pursuing retreats far and wide to begin. Simply sit back, unwind, and inhale where you are.

Reflection should be possible whenever, anyplace, and for any time allotment. Regardless of whether you're investigating contemplation just because or are a standard professional, it's imperative to remain adaptable in your methodology. Making training that works for you is vital, and you'll likely change and alter your training to suit your developing needs.

Continue perusing to learn four diverse contemplation positions, how to keep up the right stance, and the sky is the limit from there.

Seat sitting reflection

You can without much of a stretch ruminate while sitting in a seat, making this the ideal practice for noontime restoration while at work. You can ponder at work or while voyaging.

To get in the correct situation to think, sit in your seat with a straight back and with your feet level on the floor. They should shape a 90-degree edge with your knees. You may need to hurry to the edge of the seat.

Sit upright, so your head and neck are in accordance with your spine. You may put a pad behind your lower back or under your hips for included help.

On the off chance that you aren't sure how to manage your hands, you can lay them on your knees or spot them in your lap.

Standing reflection

In case you're increasingly agreeable upstanding, take a stab at standing reflection.

To do this, stand tall with your feet shoulder-width separated. Move your feet with the goal that your impact points turn marginally internal and your toes are pointing somewhat away from one another.

When you're in position, somewhat twist your knees. Enable your body to root down through your feet with each breathe out. Envision your vitality lifting out through the crown of your head with each breathe in.

For included unwinding, place your hands on your midsection with the goal that you can feel your breath traveling through your body.

Stooping contemplation

In case you're in a spot where you can serenely bow down, check out it. One favorable position of this posture is that it's simpler to keep your back straight.

To do this, lay on the floor on twisted knees. Your shins ought to be level on the floor with your lower legs underneath your base. You can put a pad between your base and heels for more help and less strain on your knees. You shouldn't feel torment when you're in this position. On the off chance that you do, attempt another reflection represent that enables you to be without torment and feel loose.

Make certain to root your weight back and down through your hips. This prevents you from putting an excessive amount of weight on your knees.

Resting reflection

You may think that it's simpler to unwind and discharge strain in the event that you rest. Along these lines, your body is completely upheld.

To do this, lie on your back with your arms stretched out close by your body. Your feet ought to be hip-separation separated, and your toes can be gone out to the side.

On the off chance that this is awkward, change the posture to help your lower back. Spot a pad underneath your knees to somewhat raise them while lying level. You can likewise twist your knees and spot your feet level on the ground.

Connection among contemplation and stance

The stance is basic to contemplation, however, you can adopt an adaptable strategy to it. Start your training while in a place that falls into place without any issues for you. It's imperative to begin in an agreeable spot, with the goal that you can tenderly move your body into the right situating all through your training.

You may find that keeping up a particular stance encourages you to set a positive aim or resolve for your training. At the point when you return to the stance or position, you can help yourself to remember why you're rehearsing — to be available, to feel loose, or whatever else you may require.

Seven-point reflection act

The seven-point reflection act is a way to deal with sitting while at the same time ruminating. There are seven rules that you can use to help accurately situate your body. Obviously, you're free to modify whatever doesn't work for you. Approach the training in a similar way that you approach your stance. Your body is effectively connected with, yet there is a non-abrasiveness to it.

1. Sitting

Contingent upon how adaptable your hips are, you can sit in the quarter, half, or full lotus position. You can likewise sit leg over the leg with your hips raised higher than your heels by sitting on a contemplation pad, towel, pad, or seat. You can utilize a pad or reflection seat to get support in many positions. It's critical to pick a representative that is agreeable so you can concentrate on your reflection.

2. Spine

Regardless of how you sit, your spine ought to be as straight as could be allowed. On the off chance that you will in general sluggard forward or influence somewhat in reverse, right now is an ideal opportunity to delicately remind yourself to return into the right stance.

Keep on establishing down through your body with each breathe out. Lift your body up and protract your spine with each breathe in. Feel the line of vitality that goes from the base of your spine out through the crown of your head. Keeping your spine straight will assist you with staying alert.

3. Hands

You can lay your hands on your thighs with your palms looking down. Keeping your hands set down is said to be additionally establishing and help loosen up your body's vitality stream.

You can likewise stack your hands in your lap with your palms looking up. To do this, place your correct hand over your left hand with your thumbs delicately contacting. This hand position is said to create more warmth and vitality.

4. Shoulders

Keep your shoulders loose and agreeable as your step them somewhat back and down. This helps keep your heart focus open and your back solid.

During your training, check in with your stance every now and then. Guarantee that your spine is straight and draw the highest points of your shoulders down and away from your ears. Focus on the tallness of your shoulders and notice in the event that one feels higher than the other with the goal that you can modify varying.

5. Jaw

Keep your jaw took care of marginally while keeping up the length in the rear of your neck. Effectively situating your jawline causes you to keep up your stance. Keep your face loose. You may find that turning the sides of your face up somewhat discharges any strain in the face.

6. Jaw

Attempt to discharge any strain you're holding in your jaw. It might be useful to keep your jaw somewhat open as you press your tongue against the top of your mouth. This consequently loosens up the jaw, takes into account clear breathing, and hinders the gulping procedure.

You can likewise do a couple of misrepresented yawns before you ponder to extend your jaw and discharge strain.

7. Look

A great many people think that it's simpler to reflect with shut eyes. Abstain from pressing your eyes shut. Delicately shutting them will assist you with keeping your face, eyes, and eyelids loose.

You can likewise reflect with open eyes. Keep up an unfocused look on the floor a couple of feet in front of you. Keep your face loose and abstain from squinting.

Choose what direction you'll think before you start, so you're not exchanging to and fro among open and shut eyes. This can be confusing and upset about the progression of your training.

Things To Remember

You may find that your contemplation practice is progressively helpful in the event that you do the accompanying:

- ❖ Start with shorter practices, and increment as you feel good.
- ❖ Focus on your breath moving in and out through your body.
- ❖ Keep your breath moderate, relentless, and smooth.
- ❖ Observe all considerations, emotions, and sensations as they emerge and pass.
- ❖ Remember that these can be sure, negative, and unbiased.
- ❖ Gently take your brain back to the present without judgment when it meanders.
- ❖ Be aware of the quietness and stillness inside.
- ❖ Bring your attention to the sounds around you individually.
- ❖ Feel the air or garments contacting your skin and feel your body contacting the floor.

Regardless, it's significant that you're cherishing and delicate with yourself. There is no incorrect method to ruminate, and what you need to escape training is altogether up to you.

What comes straightaway

Choose in the event that you need to focus on contemplation practice. Start with a feasible time, for example, 10 minutes every day, and pick the hour of the day that best suits you. Early morning and night are regularly prescribed, as contemplation can help set the pace for your day or assist you with slowing down into dozing.

It's extraordinary on the off chance that you can contemplate each day, however, it's alright on the off chance that you don't. Your way to deal with training ought to be custom-fitted to your individual needs. It might be useful to keep a concise diary to record any bits of knowledge that emerge during your training.

Remain careful and take your mindfulness back to the present minute for the duration of the day.

You may wish to look for the direction of a yoga instructor who can assist you with developing your training. There are likewise a lot of guided contemplations accessible on the web.

CHAPTER EIGHT: ARRIVING AT A MEDITATIVE STATE

It's not hard to do, yet it requires practice to figure out how to ponder. At the point when Scott Young, visitor essayist for ZenHabits, first began utilizing reflection he thought that it was hard to hold a visual scene for a time allotment without permitting diverting musings enter. With persistence, he composes that he's gotten better at holding center and removing interruptions. Here are a few hints from Scott on the best way to go into a thoughtful state:

1. Get into a position where you don't feel inconvenience however aren't totally loose. I don't mess with turning into a human pretzel. The significance is that you shouldn't have to divert solid

pressures in your body that break your center, yet in the event that you get too agreeable you may nod off. I, for the most part, sit upstanding on my bed or a cushion.

2. Close your eyes and screen your relaxing. It takes a couple of moments to enter a thoughtful state. Concentrate on taking in and out and gradually bringing down your pace of relaxing. I can here and there go to twenty seconds for a solitary breath. This wipes out interruptions as well as it powers your pulse down and loosens up your body.

3. When you've adequately eased back your breathing, start with some brisk mental activities. Run your concentration around your body. Notice where your hands, feet, elbows, and back are. Notice how they feel. In your casual express, this will additionally hone your concentration and drive out interruptions.

4. At long last attempt a couple of representation practices perceiving to what extent and how unmistakably you can hold an image, sound or sensation in your creative mind. I find once I can hold a picture for around ten or fifteen seconds with enough lucidity, I proceed onward to the reason I had for the contemplation.

This whole procedure of getting into a thoughtful state just takes me around five to ten minutes. In the event that you need practice, have a go at getting into a thoughtful state when you are resting. It will assist you with unwinding and won't remove up any additional time from your day.

Planning

As though contemplating isn't sufficiently hard, planning for it may appear to be a mammoth errand. In any case, specialists state that when you set up your body and brain before you dive into the condition of complete rest, you make certain to have an incredible session. So these are a couple of profound contemplation methods that you can do as you gear up.

1. Quiet Your Breath And Body

The breath, psyche, and body are altogether interconnected. At the point when you loosen up your body and quiet your breathing, your psyche consequently quiets down. At the point when this occurs, the parasympathetic sensory system is actuated, and thusly, the reaction to stretch is controlled.

The Easy Way

Sit in a thoughtful stance and inhale multiple times. You should ensure you take in from the nose and inhale out from your mouth. Likewise, the breaths must be profound and long. At the point when you take in, you should make yourself mindful of the present. At the point when you inhale out, loosen up every one of the muscles in your body, and simply let go. Relinquish your stresses and agony. As you do this, give extraordinary consideration to your tongue, jaw, throat, and brow.

The Right Way

You should rehearse a couple of yoga asanas and help up your body. Take 10 minutes, and do each post to its full articulation.

These are a few asanas that will help loosen up your brain:

1. SetuBandhasana
2. Dhanurasana
3. Balasana
4. AdhoMukhaSvanasana
5. ArdhaMatsyendrasana
6. Uttanasana
7. SuptaMatsyendrasana
8. Padmasana

9. Shavasana

When you have polished these asanas, you should do some breathing activities.

You should ensure that the span of breathing out is longer than taking in. Along these lines, on the off chance that you take in for four seconds, inhale out for eight. You can likewise attempt these time blends: 3-6, 5-10, 6-12, etc. Ensure you inhale tenderly. The key is to be agreeable, so tune in to your body as you go on.

2. Ensure Your Mind Is Happy

Our mind's greatest plan is to maintain a strategic distance from agony and search for joy. Along these lines, as you set yourself up for reflection, attempt to create sentiments of happiness, solidness, and security. You should promise your mind that everything is great with the goal that it isn't eager.

A cheerful personality is peaceful and arranged, so your point must be to fulfill your psyche. This is the manner by which you can do it:

1. Think of the things you are thankful for.
2. If you have had a decent thoughtful encounter, think about that.
3. Assure yourself that everything is great right now.
4. Feel great about the consistent recuperating and development that is going on.
5. If you have confidence in God, you can say a supplication before you ponder.

Search for a tranquil spot to ruminate, away from your telephone, pets, kids, and so on. At the point when you ruminate, it is your time. Tell everybody around you that.

3. Set Your Intentions And Affirmations

You should concentrate on your goal before you dive into contemplation. It will do ponders for you. You have to have a solid goal, however, to help through with it. Your insistence can be on these lines – "For the following X minutes, I will just concentrate on my contemplation. There is nothing else for me to do, and nothing else for me to consider during this time. Psyche, kindly don't upset me. I will begin focusing now."

Assurance is the way to reflect. On the off chance that you don't have it, don't stress. Practice makes you great

Practice

Presently, that you are prepared to start your reflective session, these are a couple of things you should remember.

4. Acknowledge The Distractions

As a learner, you will undoubtedly get diverted by negative considerations when you reflect. Try not to drive yourself to think positive. Acknowledge those considerations without censoring yourself. An analysis is destructive, and not in accordance with the great soul of the training.

Be delicate on yourself. It is you who instructed yourself to get diverted, thus, you should give your mind some an opportunity to prepare to be engaged. Be caring and patient with yourself.

5. Cheer The Concentration

In the event that you utilize an item to enable you to center, there will come when your brain is excessively centered around that article. Try not to stress over it. Simply appreciate how stable the brain gets as it focuses on that item.

The mind's essential capacity is to look for bliss and drive away torment and enduring. At the point when you show your mind how to think, you likewise train it to discover satisfaction with the center.

Buddhism lectures that bliss and satisfaction are two of the five elements of reflective retention. At the point when you figure out how to make the most of your contemplation, your psyche is less eager.

So when your focus is as yet creating, utilize a central article. When it gets steady, don't upset it. Simply stay where you are.

CHAPTER NINE: KEEPING UP THE MEDITATIVE STATE, COMMON BEGINNERS MISTAKES

You realize that contemplation has a few advantages, yet at times you stress that you may be committing some reflection errors, in light of the fact that your reflection isn't advancing so well. "Goodness, my reflection isn't working any longer… "

Possibly you reflect once in a while, or even each day, yet you don't feel that your contemplation is unfurling just as you anticipated. Maybe you even feel that your contemplation quit working, and are searching for approaches to cross the level.

You are not the only one.

1. You Don't Rehearse It Reliably

Of the considerable number of reasons, this is the most widely recognized!

Reflection should be drilled day by day, for it to have a genuine effect on your life. Obviously, every time you stay there is some advantage – regardless of whether just simply physical -, whether you see it or not. Be that as it may, mental and enthusiastic change just accompanies reliable practice.

So consistency ought to be your essential center when beginning or growing a contemplation practice – and not the length you sit, or how well you can create your legs. Ten minutes ordinary is superior to thirty minutes three times each week.

You utilize your psyche during all your waking hours. So your molded examples of contemplations and feelings are being strengthened day in and day out.

That is the reason it's significant that you fortify your contemplation aptitudes consistently too.

2. You Expect A Lot Of Too Early

It's alright that what kicked you off with reflection was the desire for its few advantages. Be that as it may, when you have just assembled the propensity, attempt to relinquish all desires, and basically do the training for the good of its own. Much the same as you scrub down, eat and rest each day.

How To Make That Outlook Move?

Start getting a charge out of the training itself. Appreciate the manner in which it feels after you have sat – how you get more settled, more clear, progressively focused. Obviously, reflection probably won't feel like that constantly, yet on the off chance that you have been rehearsing it sufficiently long, you will comprehend that in normal it feels very great.

A large number of the more profound reflection benefits come simply after months or long periods of everyday practice. So holding your desires softly is an unquestionable requirement, so you can remain with it for the long stretch.

3. You Don't Get Ready Before You Practice

You can just sit and begin your contemplation, whenever of the day, as a great many people do. However, your session can go a lot further in the event that you take only a few minutes all ready to loosen up your body, quiet your breath, and certify your goal.

It tends to be as basic as simply doing two or three stretches, taking three full breaths, and confirming your goal, "alright, I will concentrate now".

4. You Hop From Method To Strategy

In the main months of your contemplation practice, it's alright to attempt various methods or to do an alternate guided reflection consistently. Be that as it may, after some time you need to pick a specific procedure and stick to it.

Various individuals improve various procedures. So it's critical to try different things with various strategies until you find what works best for you. Maybe you can attempt one for 1 a month, to get an underlying "feel" for it before proceeding onward to another if the contemplation isn't directly for you. That is the thing that I have finished with more than 70 styles of reflection!

It's significant, toward the end, to discover one system for yourself, and afterward stay with it.

This is particularly the situation for fixation contemplation. With every session you do with a similar item—suppose your breath or a mantra—that article turns out to be increasingly "charged" with consideration. Your psyche turns out to be increasingly cozy with it, in a manner of speaking. This partiality, thusly, makes it simpler to keep up center around that article in future sessions.

5. You Continue Questioning In The Event That You Are Doing It Right

Since you care about your training and need to improve, you may tend to overanalyze it. This was an impediment to my very own training for quite a while. It's an error that can take unobtrusive structures, so we should be cognizant not to participate in this kind of mental masturbation.

The issue with self-assessing your training an excess of is two-overlap:

- ❖ It keeps your mind caught up with, during the training, with examining your psychological states, as opposed to being in the reflection procedure
- ❖ It regularly demotivates you, when you can't locate a good response to the inquiry "Am I

doing this right?". On the off chance that you presume that you are not doing it right, or you can't make sense of it, you are probably going to surrender.

So you have to release that and simply practice. Time will realize you clearness the reflection procedure, as it turns out to be a greater amount of an encounter for you as opposed to something you have to comprehend and portray.

Keep hungry, continue learning, continue trying different things with inconspicuous contrasts in your methodologies. In the event that you have a decent contemplation educator or a network, at that point suggest your conversation starters as clear as you can and see what you can realize. However, realize that you should continue pushing ahead, regardless of your vulnerabilities.

Trust me, things get more clear with time and practice.

Comprehend that reflection is a basic two-advance procedure:

❖ Step 1: put your consideration on the reflection item, and keep it there for whatever length of time that you can

❖ Step 2: notice when you get diverted, when you can, and rehash stage one

Your essential objective is just to see as fast as you can when an interruption occurs. Possibly in your first weeks, your brain may frequently meander for 2-5 minutes before you even understand that it has meandered. Step by step makes this hole shorter, by being increasingly mindful of what's going on within you. This is care.

Your optional objective is to keep your consideration, a great many minutes, on your contemplation object. To start with you might have the option to do that for just 3-5 seconds, yet with time and practice, it increments. This is fixation. Devices like the Muse

Headband can assist you with having a better understanding of how well you are concentrating.

On the off chance that you do these two things just as you can, at that point you are doing it right! CAnd in the event that you might want to more readily comprehend the mechanics of reflection, look at my post on the procedure of contemplation.

CHAPTER TEN:
UTILIZE YOUR BREATHE TO CALM YOUR MIND AND MASTER YOUR EMOTIONS

Sentiments or feelings like dread, outrage, bitterness, blame, disgrace, question, etc, are exceptionally ground-breaking powers. At the point when left to go crazy, they can make us state or do things that we lament. Furthermore, when kept in or held down, they can putrefy as sickness and malady. They can deaden us or engage us. They can quietness us or drive us to progress.

Feelings are exceptionally sound and normal energies. What's more, similar to all energies, they are intended to stream. Sentiments and feelings mean we are alive. They are not intended to be halted, blocked, or stifled.

Also, they are not intended to be utilized as weapons to hurt ourselves or others. On the off chance that we lash out or venture our awkward feelings, we can hurt others. In the event that we smother or stifle them, we can hurt ourselves. No big surprise such a significant number of good individuals grapple with their emotions.

Enthusiastic vitality resembles a fire. Deliberately tended, it can warm us and support us. Left uncontrolled, it can consume our home and our life down! No big surprise such a large number of good individuals battle to express their sentiments and feelings. No big surprise such a large number of individuals just contain them.

At the workshops recently, we have been building up our normal capacity to inhale into our sentiments and to channel our feelings through the breath. It is astounding what happens when we figure out how to utilize the breath to meet and welcome whatever sentiments and feelings emerge in us.

We locate that behind, under, or inside all feelings is unadulterated life power vitality, and we can figure out how to incorporate or divert this vitality in groundbreaking, positive and beneficial ways.

Directing these amazing energies is an ability that takes practice. However, it is one that merits acing, in light of the fact that these amazing energies can serve us and the world limitlessly.

The breathing mantra we use in this act of diverting, coordinating or changing passionate vitality is: "open and extend" (that is the breath in), and unwind and let go (that is the breath out). What's more, for reasons unknown, this is fundamentally a cognizant and conscious moan of help. The moan of help (additionally called a purging breath is a center procedure in Breathwork. It is a mystery to getting to the normal mending and inventive intensity of our feelings. You can figure out how to utilize your breath along these lines to innovatively channel your feelings or to securely vent them.

The other center procedure is "associated breathing," likewise called "constant" or "round" relaxing. Rehearsing these two center breathwork strategies will assist you with rooting out and discharge undesirable propensities and designs, and to liberate you from excruciating sentiments and stifled feelings.

Have you seen the impact that incredible feelings have on the body? It worries. The throat closes as the neck, jaw, brow, chest, stomach area and different muscles will in general agreement or respond. Maybe the body is attempting to get away, evade, or secure itself against its own feelings and sentiments!

Our old progenitors were more likely than not discovered that communicating ground-breaking feelings can be extremely perilous. It appears that we have built up an oblivious propensity or design, or an inclination to stifle or contain them. At the point when we become sincerely stimulated, initiated or agitated, amazing synthetic compounds are delivered and discharged into the framework. Furthermore, it typically takes one to three minutes for these synthetic concoctions to run their course before we "return to our faculties" once more.

Thus, the game is to figure out how to deal with ourselves or our feelings during those initial hardly any crucial points in time of enactment. What's more, that is actually where Breathwork comes in. At the point when we figure out how to just unwind and feel our sentiments when we learn to inhale into our emotions and to channel our feelings into the breath, we get liberated from them, we take the pressure of the body-mind framework.

Will surviving, incorporating or exploring amazing wild feelings be that simple? Would it be able to be that basic? All things considered, the appropriate response is yes! It is an aptitude, and it essentially takes practice.

Furthermore, obviously, how we outline things is likewise significant. For instance, it is helpful to comprehend that tension is true 'energy'. Furthermore, a superior word for pressure is 'challenge'. Taking a gander at it along these lines enables us to move toward things in an unexpected way, and this reframing can open ways to progressively inventive arrangements. The exercise here is to rehearse these two center systems when incredible sentiments and feelings emerge. What's more, obviously, it pays to rehearse when you feel serene and quiet. It resembles working on gliding or swimming in the shallow finish of the pool before plunging into the sea.

There is a particular sort of opportunity that accompanies the capacity to inhale into our sentiments and channel feelings into the breath. Life is quite a lot more fun and pleasant when we are not pushed and pulled or deadened by dread and outrage, or misery or uncertainty. A specific straightforwardness and elegance stream into our lives when we can open and extend and to unwind and give up as opposed to fixing and contracting or naturally responding when amazing life energies stir in us.

You might be shocked at how little practice it takes to change your pressure and tension into opportunity and straightforwardness. Thus, I recommend you practice.

Give yourself an extensive breathe in and a loose breathe out the present moment. Do it a couple of times and notice how rapidly this can initiate sentiments and sensations in your body. Work on breathing and unwinding into these sentiments and sensations.

Practice at whatever point you end up getting pushed or pulled cockeyed sincerely or mentally.

Ace the two center breath work procedures and use them to defeat negative, useless or self-undermining propensities and examples and responses. Practice with positive sentiments just as negative ones, minimal ones just as large ones, since they all contain vitality that can be utilized to elevate, reinforce, calm, balance, stimulate or recharge yourself. With training, you can lift yourself up or quiet yourself down. You can utilize the breath to stay clear and cherishing, tranquil and imaginative, even in the most energizing and testing snapshots of your life!

CHAPTER ELEVEN: CONSCIOUSNESS OF YOUR BODY AND ENVIRONMENT AROUND YOU

Breathing contemplation is the broadest sort of consideration practice, and fundamental so as to perform different sorts of consideration practice. It will consequently, in general, be the most usually drilled and early on of structures. In any case, essential however it might be, acing contemplation requires the same amount of order and expertise as acing some other practice, so it would be a misstep to think of it as fundamentally simpler or less progressed than different practices.

While meditators may appear to the outside eyewitness to just be unwinding, quite certain psychological exercise is occurring inside. An individual may appear to be actually the equivalent in two sessions yet may have had a magnificent achievement in one session, and performed inadequately in another. It is typical for starting meditators to discover contemplation trying and troublesome. From the start, they may even think about what the serious deal is. Be that as it may, after some time, recognizable improvement is made, and you will know it in your session as you accomplish further levels. The improvement will likewise show outside your session as a more noteworthy capacity to focus, the profundity of consideration, center, and true serenity. The capacity to center consideration and increment mindfulness is the thing that takes into account more prominent inward and external care – and these capacities are primary to numerous different practices, just as the general undertaking to disguise numerous thoughtful lessons from minor information to an increasingly instinctive level.

Reason

The essential reason is basic: our undeveloped personalities, by and large, will in general skip from point to the subject, state to state. This kind of affiliated hopping about is called 'monkey mind' by the Buddhists. It is truly recognizable in youngsters, yet grown-ups, for the most part, experience the ill effects of it too.

Indeed, even extremely astute individuals (now and then particularly keen individuals) will, in general, ruminate over a wide range of things interminably. This is only from time to time a matter of productive 'performing various tasks'. Or maybe, it is a kind of wandering off in fantasy land that, best case scenario, brings about an absence of center and being 'somewhere else' than the present. At the very least, ruminations can be a wellspring of incredible disappointment and stress. In either case, care is beyond the realm of imagination in such a state since care includes consistent familiarity with one's self, one's considerations and emotions, one's condition, and one's circumstance in the present, both inner and outside.

Contemplation enables us to improve our capacity to intentionally coordinate our consideration where we conclude it will go, and for to what extent. This is done a lot of like working out a muscle. In reflection, we select something consistent whereupon to center. Truly outstanding and most seasoned things to choose is the breath – in light of the fact that regardless of your conditions, your breath is consistent with you as long as you are alive.

Position

To start with, it is essential to consider your body position. A great many people have seen meditators situated with legs crossed, hands either collapsed in the lap or improved and settling upon the knees, and a straight stance. These customary positions may work for some individuals however we are not all that worried about anyone's explicit position. The key concern, rather, is this: you ought to sit in a way that (an) enables you to inhale effectively, (b) permits your body enough solace that you can stay in that position all through your reflection without your body turning into an interruption, and (c) isn't happy to such an extent that it urges you to nod off.

It is in this manner not suggested that you think while resting. Some may decide to sit in a seat, however, the seat ought to enable your stance to be sufficiently straight to inhale well – not slumped. Sitting upright is one region where starting muscle uneasiness will merit the act of figuring out how to keep up the stance. Concerning legs, molding after some time may empower you to get equipped for sitting on the floor with them crossed if that is as of now awkward. In any case, that is a different physical practice and try – particular from multiple points of view from the act of contemplation in essence.

Along these lines, a situated meditator can become as capable at the reflection as a leg over leg meditator. Once more, paying little mind to the position, the fundamental issues are that it permits great breathing, isn't diverting, and won't make you nod off. Basically, you should utilize a stance that will enable you to 'disregard your body' during the term of your reflection.

Individuals contemplate with eyes open or close, yet shut is commonly the liked. Further, when closing your eyes, it will be essential to learn not to imagine different symbolism (something that can be trying from the outset for visual masterminds). Rather, the vision ought to just be 'turned off', including inner 'mental dreams'.

The mouth can be somewhat open with the jaw hanging free. A decent situation for the tongue can be let free, yet contacting the rear of the two front teeth and top of the mouth, yet this may differ for people. Once more, the key ought to be unwinding and no interruption.

Reflection Aides

You will likewise need to consider to what extent you will reflect. 15 minutes might be a decent measure of time for novices; for somewhere in the range of 20 minutes might be perfect. You can inevitably work for as long as 30 minutes. Some ruminate longer, however on the off chance that you need to set up an everyday schedule it is essential to choose something sensible and manageable inside your calendar. You'll have to set up an approach to caution yourself when the time is up. This should be possible essentially with a stopwatch, a kitchen clock, and so on. In the event that you are in a guided reflection, the guide will alarm you. There are cell phone reflection applications that enable you to set a period and have a decent loosening up ring sounds to look over. There are likewise online recordings accessible with guided reflections highlighting voices, music, and so forth. Anyway, it is accomplished, a basic toll after an assigned time is presumably best for novices.

A few people light incense when thinking or performing different ceremonies. The olfactory sense (smell) is one of the most personally associated faculties with our memory focuses. Along these lines, having an uncommon fragrance is a decent method to move our perspective into one that is helpful for the focal point of the custom or practice.

Different pads and furniture might be wanted by some relying upon the setting and position you pick, yet be careful with being convinced into spending a lot of cash on pointless things. A few people may get a kick out of the chance to have little models or pictures of individuals or subjects which move them or help them to remember different qualities or standards, or just make a charming situation, yet these too are not carefully vital for contemplation. It's up to you!

With your surroundings set up and your physical position is chosen, you are currently prepared to start.

Body Scan

The initial segment of the procedure ought to be a psychological survey of your body to guarantee you are really loosening up it. Regularly we hold muscles firmly gripped without acknowledging it. In this manner, you should take a profound long breath and let it out through your nose. Presently envision the highest point of your head being checked. As the line around your head descends over your face, your muscles here ought to unwind: first the sanctuaries, temple, forehead; next to your cheeks, jaw muscles, ears, neck, and so on. Move the enclosing line down over your neck, shoulders, down your arms to your fingers, down your back, stomach, legs, feet, and toes – loosening up each gathering as you go. Try not to go too rapidly so you may think about all zones. In the event that you believe you have to, you can gradually come back to the highest point of your head.

Presently take one all the more full breath and discharge your consideration from your body. From hereafter, your breathing ought not to be controlled – simply let yourself breathe in and out naturally without attempting to guide it, paying little mind to how quick, slow, profound, shallow, standard, or unpredictable that is.

Centering

Presently, keeping your eyes shut, concentrate on your breath. There will be a compulsion to control your breath or attempt to make it customary or more profound, however, you ought to dodge that allurement.

Essentially watch your breath without guiding it. It is significant not to attempt to coordinate or control the breath, however, let the body do it. It may be profound or shallow, quick or moderate, and may change over the contemplation – and that is alright. Once more, basically, watch without coordinating. The segment you should focus in on is the air moving simply past the edge of your noses, as it moves in and out. You will hear it and feel it moving and as you watch without coordinating a partition will shape so it is progressively similar to the floods of the sea upon the shoreline, coming in and out. Attempt to concentrate solely on that experience without contemplating it in 'words'. Additionally disregard any representations, sensations from your body, or different considerations. This is an unadulterated experience, instead of our confining of it.

After you breathe out, in the event that you are refreshed, there will presumably be a couple of moments before your body normally instigates the following inward breath. This will be the most enticing minute for contemplations to interfere. Let your psyche stay as still in that space as could reasonably be expected. Your body will at that point give the following inward breath and line it as far as possible up with your consideration, etc. Try not to leave the present minute or consider to what extent it's been or to what extent you need to go. Without referencing past or future, your experience may at times become 'ageless'.

Meandering and Correction

As you endeavor reflection, your mind will definitely meander. Things will fly into your head, for example, the day's to-do things, what others around you may be doing or thinking, what the arbitrary little sounds you're hearing may be, physical uneasiness, fascinating or irregular recollections, or maybe all the more concerning ruminations about different life issues. As this occurs and you get yourself, seeing you have been occupied from the breath, it is significant not to frame decisions about the interruptions around you or contemplations and sentiments inside. Mood killer your judgment-machine for the time being.

These decisions of good/terrible, ought/shouldn't are what make interruptions all the more diverting. The explanation flying creatures tweeting outside don't occupy us as much as two individuals contending is a result of our judgment that one is excellent and the other irritating.

[176]

Rather, when you get yourself, just return your concentrate only to your breath. In the event that you didn't do this, at that point reflection would not be not normal for fantasizing or clear dreaming. Maybe a decent undertaking in its own particular manners, however not the consideration building impact of careful reflection. As these things emerge in your brain, don't overlook or stifle them, however essentially consider them to be articles and put them in a safe spot, moving your concentrate tenderly back to the breath.

In spite of your earnest attempts, your mind will do this multiple occasions and should be taken back to the breath ordinarily. Similarly as significant as getting and guiding yourself back, it is additionally fundamental that you did not let this disappoint you. Keep in mind, contemplating the way that you're not considering your breath is additionally 'pondering an option that is other than your breath'. Rather, essentially take your consideration back to your breath as if it were a single errand – without disappointment in view of past needs to do as such, and without exacerbation in light of dread of expecting to do it again later on. As you ponder there is just the present, and in that present just the breath. Try not to think about this meandering as an 'inability to ponder' or as an exemption to contemplation. The meandering, and the accompanying redresses in the center, are all piece of reflection – all is similarly as it ought to be.

Tallying

On the off chance that you are having an especially anxious personality today, or at a beginning period of training, you may think that it's accommodating to check your breaths. This is a marking and encircling with language so it isn't exactly the perfect of unadulterated experience. Be that as it may, similar to a mantra, it tends to be a useful instrument to keep our consideration set up. I consider it the 'preparation wheels' of contemplation, and even experienced meditators may require or favor it on occasion.

On the off chance that you do check, do it along these lines: as you breathe in don't think anything – simply center around the inward breath. At that point, as you breathe out, think, "one… " You can think this word as enduring as long as they breathe out, as yet concentrating consideration reporting in real-time moving out of your noses. Ensure you don't breathe out the whole distance and afterward think "one" soon after – that is naming a past memory, not remaining in this very microsecond as it's going on.

Rather, "Ooooooonnnnneee" ought to follow the breath right down. Next, as you take in, attempt to think nothing in the middle of other than essentially watching the internal breath. Breathing out, think, "two… " Go up to five and afterward come back to one. This example follows our mind's common desire for talking on the breathe out.

Coincidentally, coming back to 1 in the included in a cycle is significant. On the off chance that you don't return in this cycle from 5 back to 1 and rather proceed to higher numbers, it will be simple for the tallying to wind up on 'autopilot' as your mind strays to different things. The arrival is the sign that you truly are giving close consideration to the tallying. Moreover, in the event that you neglect to stay concentrated on your breath, you can endeavor to just get past one entire cycle 1-5, along these lines making the test one of scaled-down lumps. At that point, you can endeavor another cycle – continually staying in the present.

Going Deeper

Despite the fact that a meandering personality and the need to address its concentration back to breathing is not out of the ordinary, after some time you will turn out to be better ready to keep your consideration on your breath with no different contemplations emerging and for longer timeframes between mental wanderings. This expansion in capacity is recognizable inside sessions, yet additionally proceeds from session to session on the off chance that you practice contemplation routinely.

With that expanded capacity to look after consideration, comes different impacts during the time you are in a reflection session. These include more noteworthy ecological mindfulness, loss of body, and cognizance separation.

The first, and most effortless to see, is more prominent natural mindfulness. During a reflection, you come to see the entirety of the little and unobtrusive sounds and sensations around you – the clock ticking, winged animals, vehicles driving by, the breeze, individuals talking out there, etc. The reality of this mindfulness as you progress may appear to be opposing since these things can be interruptions which cause you to need to reset your emphasis back on your breath. While that is valid, it is likewise evident that before you were contemplating a large number of these things would have gone totally unnoticed by you.

The explanation you notice them during your session is an indication that your brain is getting still. Toss a rock into a stormy sea and its belongings are lost, yet in a still lake, it's far-reaching influences are critical. While the impression of these beforehand unnoticed things is surely another arrangement of contemplations to be saved so the center can come back to the breath, they are additionally an indication of progress in light of the fact that a still personality is one of the points of reflection.

The second impact you may understand during a session may take some training, maybe more than a few sessions, before you begin to get looks at it. Loss of body is, obviously, an allegorical portrayal. Yet, the general sensation will be an absence of impression of the body; it's little hurts, tingles, small developments, and so on. This will achieve a sentiment of separation from the body, yet is basically the aftereffect of outrageous core interest. In any case, this inclination – when it occurs – is an indication of progress in your strategy.

The dubious thing about the loss of the body is that it isn't just uncommon from the start, however, it will, in general, be brief. In the event that one is deliberately centered around attempting to have lost body understanding, at that point, it is unthinkable, as the experience results from an absence of calculated reasoning. When the experience occurs, it regularly closes rapidly. Generally, when an individual starts to see that they are encountering lost body sensation, its seeing makes the mind put a name on it, and transform the experience into a psychological article. The minute you believe, "I'm having lost body understanding!" you have now lost your core interest. Previously, you had started to enter a condition of understanding without language and marks and without qualifications between things. Be that as it may, calling your brain to think about the loss of body experience makes a qualification among it and different encounters, and among you and your condition. Definitely, the entirety of the standard ideas floods over into your awareness. The mind hopes to check whether the body is there and, obviously, it is. Your mind starts 'checking the post box' to check whether any messages (sensations) from the body have shown up – which, obviously, they have.

In any case, such as everything else, the psyche improves after some time. With nonstop practice, these encounters become increasingly visit, simpler to enter and last more.

Another experience you may have during intercession may be called cognizance separation. We, as people, are comprised of numerous capacities and properties (totals) which, cooperating in complex connections, yield a general impression of 'self' which we consider as 'us'. These incorporate memory, feelings, coherent capacity, determination abilities, observations, and that's only the tip of the iceberg. Be that as it may, on the off chance that we were to gradually envision these properties stripping endlessly, and if we somehow managed to take a gander at them exclusively, there is nobody property we could convincingly recognize as 'us'. We are, fairly, a component of these exercises. Another of these totals is cognizance. This isn't such a great amount of familiarity with certain data, (for example, attention to our environment or of the substance of our contemplations). Or maybe, this is the genuine first-individual experience of 'similarity' – i.e., what it is 'like' to be an encountering being. One may envision easier creatures or bugs having this sentiment of what it resembles to be them, without the advancement of incorporated recollections of any intricacy. Some awareness logicians and nervous system specialists call this sensation qualia.

After an individual desert every other vibe of body, their environment, and other substantial musings, their brains enter another state. Here they experience that awareness in a totally disconnected structure, without the typical going with musings, emotions, suppositions, decisions, recollections, marks, sensations, concerns, and different impressions. They essentially 'exist'. Here it is said one can encounter the universe 'as it actually is' deprived of our standard encircling of it.

Prompt After Effects

What present moment eventual outcomes would one be able to anticipate from a quality contemplation session? The most fundamental impact is a loose and low-stress state, typically joined by a feeling of tolerance, happiness, and agreeableness. Notwithstanding these, the mind will be significantly more engaged, controllable, and deliberative. If one somehow managed to watch a speaker soon after, for instance, it is simpler to concentrate on the speaker for an all-inclusive period, while every other interruption would be effectively saved. If one somehow happened to participate in some sort of mental undertaking, they would probably be progressively compelling at it, in an uplifted condition of fixation.

This 'laser' concentrates typically scatters after some time. As the day's exercises continue, the psyche needs to deal with more things all the while and consideration can get diffused. Certain things have an incredible propensity to diffuse consideration rapidly. Probably the best case of things that diffuse consideration is tuning in to or watching media, for example, music or TV.

Critically, you have a level of decision in how rapidly or gradually your consideration gets diffused, in light of your purpose. In the event that you intentionally start filling your psyche with various ruminations and concerns, you can diffuse your consideration more rapidly than if you attempt to stay careful and in a semi-thoughtful like quiet after your session.

Long haul Effects

Longer-term impacts are normally improved when reflection is joined with a strong rational establishment. The vast majority of the aptitudes created in contemplation identify with explicit scholarly standards and can be utilized to live these standards all the more handily throughout everyday life. In the event that reflection was just about the experience during a session, and just about more prominent concentration and stress alleviation, at that point, it would not have the significant spot in profound practice that it has had for a huge number of years. The general idea of contemplation is that, while it might start as explicit sessions, we inevitably figure out how to extend reflective care into the remainder of our lives, musings, and activities.

For example, the first of the more profound impacts referenced before, still personality, is something that can be taken into our lives as we experience our day. Past that, the capacity to see inconspicuous things that originates from a still personality can alarm us to interruptions and so forth emerging in our psyches before they can devour us. It might likewise make us progressively mindful of nuances in the conduct of others, improving our capacity to act toward them with sympathy.

Having encounters of partition from our bodies and awareness separation can cause a buzz of unity with the universe. The capacity to go into such states can make a more noteworthy propensity to see things from to a greater extent a general perspective than from the perspective of our shallow conceited point of view.

A few neuroscientists study the physiological impacts of contemplation on the mind, and these investigations have so far loaned assurance to the thought these progressions are more than insignificant misleading impact. In reflection, we have an incorporated practice-theory which includes dynamic adjustment of our neural engineering, alongside mental propensities and capacities which encourage more noteworthy use of astuteness lessons, and a more prominent combination of them into our characteristic reactions.

It is as such that care is expanded, which would then be able to add into our typical judgment focuses, and better screen our own contemplations and sentiments about things, instead of enabling them to expend us thoughtlessly.

CHAPTER TWELVE: STOMACH BREATHE RELAXATION

Have you at any point seen how you inhale when you feel loose? Whenever you are loose, pause for a minute to see how your body feels. Or on the other hand, consider how you inhale when you first get up in the first part of the day or just before you nod off. Breathing activities can enable you to unwind, on the grounds that they make your body feel like it does when you are loose.

Profound breathing is probably the most ideal approaches to bring down worry in the body. This is on the grounds that when you inhale profoundly, it makes an impression on your cerebrum to quiet down and unwind. The cerebrum at that point sends this message to your body. Those things that happen when you are pushed, for example, expanded pulse, quick breathing, and hypertension, all abatement as you inhale profoundly to unwind.

❖ The way you inhale influences your entire body. Breathing activities are a decent method to unwind, lessen pressure, and calm pressure.

❖ Breathing practices are anything but difficult to learn. You can do them at whatever point you need, and you needn't bother with any extraordinary devices or gear to do them.

❖ You can do various activities to see which work best for you.

How would you do breathing activities?

There are bunches of breathing activities you can do to help unwind. The principal practice beneath— midsection breathing—is easy to learn and simple to do. It's ideal to begin there on the off chance that you have never done breathing activities. Different activities are further developed. These activities can assist you with unwinding and ease the pressure.

Paunch Relaxing

Paunch breathing is anything but difficult to do and exceptionally unwinding. Attempt this fundamental exercise whenever you have to unwind or diminish pressure.

1. Sit or lie level in an agreeable position.
2. Put one hand on your paunch just beneath your ribs and the other hand on your chest.
3. Take a full breath in through your nose, and let your paunch drive your hand out. Your chest ought not to move.
4. Breathe out through pressed together lips as though you were whistling. Feel the hand on your midsection go in, and use it to drive all the freshen up.
5. Do this breathing 3 to multiple times. Take as much time as necessary with every breath.

6. Notice how you feel toward the finish of the activity.

Following stages

After you have aced paunch breathing, you might need to attempt one of these further developed breathing activities. Attempt each of the three, and see which one works best for you:

- ❖ 4-7-8 relaxing
- ❖ Roll relaxing
- ❖ Morning relaxing

4-7-8 Relaxing

This activity additionally utilizes gut breathing to enable you to unwind. You can do this activity either sitting or resting.

1. To beginning, put one hand on your paunch and the other on your chest as in the gut breathing activity.
2. Take a profound, slow breath from your paunch, and quietly consider to 4 you take in.

3. Hold your breath, and quietly check from 1 to 7.

4. Breathe out totally as you quietly check from 1 to 8. Attempt to get all the let some circulation into your lungs when you tally to 8.

5. Repeat 3 to multiple times or until you feel quiet.

6. Notice how you feel toward the finish of the activity.

Move relaxing

Move breathing causes you to grow full utilization of your lungs and to concentrate on the mood of your relaxing. You can do it in any position. Be that as it may, while you are learning, it is ideal to lie on your back with your knees bowed.

1. Put your left hand on your midsection and your correct hand on your chest. Notice how your hands move as you take in and out.

2. Practice filling your lower lungs by breathing so that your "midsection" (left) hand goes up when you breathe in and your "chest" (right) hand stays still. Continuously take in through your nose and inhale out through your mouth. Do this 8 to multiple times.

3. When you have filled and purged your lower lungs 8 to multiple times, add the second means to your breathing: breathe in first into your lower lungs as in the past, and afterward, keep breathing in into your upper chest. Inhale gradually and normally. As you do as such, your correct hand will rise and your left hand will fall a little as your stomach falls.

4. As you breathe out gradually through your mouth, make a calm, whooshing sound as first your left hand and afterward your correct hand fall. As you breathe out, feel the pressure leaving your body as you become increasingly loose.

5. Practice taking did thusly for 3 to 5 minutes. Notice that the development of your

midsection and chest rises and falls like the movement of moving waves.

6. Notice how you feel toward the finish of the activity.

Practice moves to breathe day by day for a little while until you can do it anyplace. You can utilize it as a moment unwinding device whenever you need one.

Alert: Some individuals get woozy the initial scarcely any occasions they attempt to move relaxing. In the event that you start to inhale excessively quick or feel discombobulated, slow you are relaxing. Get up gradually.

Early daytime relaxing

Attempt this activity when you initially get up in the first part of the day to alleviate muscle solidness and clear obstructed breathing entries. At that point use it for the duration of the day to soothe backpressure.

1. From a standing position, twist forward from the abdomen with your knees marginally bowed, letting your arms dangle near the floor.

2. As you breathe in gradually and profoundly, come back to a standing situation by moving up easing back, lifting your head last.

3. Hold your breath for only a couple of moments in this standing position.

4. Exhale gradually as you come back to the first position, bowing forward from the midriff.

5. Notice how you feel toward the finish of the activity.

CHAPTER THIRTEEN: 5 MINUTE GUIDED RELAXATION

Reflection has numerous brilliant advantages for pressure on the board. One of the most important parts of reflection is that it can manufacture flexibility after some time, however, it can likewise assist one with feeling less worried in minutes whenever utilized as an apparatus to just loosen up your body and psyche. It can likewise assist you with getting into the act of reacting to the difficulties throughout your life from an increasingly loose, careful spot as opposed to responding to life's difficulties out of dread, and it can assist you with getting in the act of relinquishing feelings of resentment and diverting yourself away from rumination.

In spite of the numerous advantages of contemplation, it very well may be a scary practice to start. Maybe shockingly, numerous individuals don't attempt reflection since they trust it's hard to rehearse or just powerful with standard, protracted sessions. False! Contemplation can be rehearsed from numerous points of view, so there will undoubtedly be an assortment of strategies that resound with every person, and with every individual's circumstance.

For instance, on the off chance that you are a shower individual, a tub reflection might be the ideal thing for your next shower; chocolate darlings may incredibly appreciate a chocolate contemplation. The individuals who like to move may favor a mobile contemplation.

And keeping in mind that you can get the greatest increases from reflection with visit practice, only five minutes of contemplation really can bring snappy pressure help. So in the event that you just have five minutes for contemplation, here's the way to make the most of them:

Steps for a Quick Meditation

1. Set aside time. Set a clock for five minutes, so you can unwind and not stress over remaining in contemplation for 'excessively long', missing arrangements. (On the off chance that you have an iPhone, the Healing Music application can be utilized as a clock, however, the normal clock that accompanies most telephones can likewise be helpful.)

2. Relax your body. Simply close your eyes and unwind. Take a couple of full breaths from your stomach and discharge the strain in your body. Attempt to envision the pressure leaving your body from your head to your feet, either as envisioning that the pressure is truly depleting from you through your toes, getting away from your body with each breath, or essentially dissolving endlessly.

3. Clear your brain. At the point when you chip away at clearing your psyche of considerations, instead of concentrating on 'considering nothing', center around 'being', and when contemplations enter your brain, delicately recognize them and let them go, restoring your concentration to the present minute once more. On the off chance that you center around how well you are getting along this, that turns into the core interest. In the event that you acknowledge that continually taking your brain back to the present minute is the contemplation, it will be a lot simpler to keep your mind still.

4. Keep going. Proceed with this for five minutes, and come back to your day feeling increasingly loose and invigorated. Just spotlight on the sensations you are feeling in your body, center around your breath, or spotlight on giving up. Attempt this contemplation normally, and you should feel less focused on in general.

Tips

1. Be sure you're in an agreeable position; small pestering inconveniences like scratchy garments or an ungainly sitting position can be an interruption from contemplation.

2. Don't get excessively centered around whether you're 'doing it right'. (This can really make reflection progressively distressing!) Thoughts may regularly enter your head; the way toward diverting your concentration to the present minute is the place the advantage comes.

3. Playing contemplation music or utilizing fragrant healing can improve your training. They aren't important, yet they can add to your experience in the event that you can advantageously join them.

4. Meditation has been utilized for both momentary quieting (it can invert your pressure reaction before long) and long haul versatility (the customary practice can assist you with getting less receptive to stretch), so

visit contemplation is a great and compelling pressure the executives' instrument.

5. For best outcomes, attempt to fit in longer reflection sessions (like 20 minutes or increasingly) a couple of times each week. At that point, you will be progressively rehearsed with reflection as a rule, and these 5-minute sessions will have a greater amount of an effect when you need them!

CHAPTER FOURTEEN: 10 MINUTE GUIDED RELAXATION

Indeed, even a short 10-minute reflection can possibly do a great deal for both your body and psyche.

Things being what they are, how would you do this short contemplation works out?

Here are a couple of things you can do to help encourage your 10-minute contemplation:

1. Find a calm space
2. Let others realize you would prefer not to be upset for the following 10 minutes
3. Find an agreeable situation to sit or lie in
4. Take a couple of profound, purging breaths
5. Set a clock or follow a guided reflection track

Does Guided Meditation Work For Anxiety?

Reflection can help with numerous emotional wellness concerns, including tension and misery.

Through reliable reflection, you can really change the science of your cerebrum through a wonder called neuroplasticity.

Contemplation has been demonstrated to effectively affect those managing nervousness and despondency. Only five minutes daily can improve things significantly.

Specifically, care contemplation has been demonstrated to be useful for those experiencing tension issues, for example, Generalized Anxiety Disorder, Post-Traumatic Stress Disorder, and Obsessive-Compulsive Disorder.

How would you practice care reflection?

Care contemplation is a type of reflection that energizes present minute mindfulness.

Perhaps the most ideal approaches to rehearse care is to just focus on the breath. Monitoring every breath as it enters and leaves the body is care. It truly is that straightforward.

In case you're new to care, why not attempt a guided reflection? It's the most ideal approach, to begin with, the training in a delicate, sound way.

Top Twelve 10-Minute Guided Meditations

1. "Guided Meditation for Gratitude"

Time: 9 Minutes

Reason: Gratitude

Appreciation is a demonstrated type of expanding satisfaction in your day by day life, however, we regularly center a lot around specifying what we are thankful for and insufficient on the genuine sentiment of appreciation. This track will assist you with feeling appreciation at a more profound level, right away and value those parts of your life you might be underestimating.

2. "Care Meditation"

Time: 10 Minutes

Reason: Mindfulness

Recorded in the calming voice of Rick Clark, this is a ground-breaking contemplation to remain still and be careful. It is tied in with watching your musings, controlling them and releasing them. It is astounding what you can achieve just by watching your considerations liberated from judgment, at that point letting them cruise by, leaving you still and plain by pessimism or stress.

3. "Positive Breathing Awareness"

Time: 10 Minutes

Object: Being Present

This is an extraordinary track in the event that you are looking for not so much direction but rather more space to inhale sit still. Being increasingly present is one of the incredible advantages of tracks that attention a great deal on breathing and taking musings back to the present.

4. "Stir Your Perfect Health"

Time: 11 Minutes

Reason: Improving your wellbeing

This track has an objective to carry care and attention to your wellbeing, by understanding that pressure is an indication of us not getting what we need. It is a quieting, sustaining piece that causes you to hinder your breath while breathing into parts of your body you need to mend.

5. "Breath Sound Meditation"

Time: 9 Minutes

Reason for existing: Being Mindfully Aware

Appreciate an unwinding exercise that will assist you with seeing your body from inside your body, while as yet staying mindful of your environment.

6. "10-Minute Breathing"

Time: 9 Minutes

Reason for existing: Being available

Much like different contemplations, this spotlights on being available and carefully mindful, while likewise unwinding. This particular track doesn't have a foundation sound or music, so you can blend it in with one of the tracks in our rundown underneath.

7. "All The Time You Need"

Time: 9 Minutes

Reason for existing: Being available

"I have constantly I need" — this amazing insistence will assist you with getting present and advise you that, whatever it is that is worrying you, you will make sense of it and you do have constantly you need.

8. "Breathing Meditation"

Time: 10 Minutes

Object: Being available

This track is likewise a calm one with no ambient melodies, and it centers for the most part around the cadence of the breath and recognizing the nearness of contemplations and emotions, and delicately breathing into that space.

9. "Brief Sitting Meditation"

Time: 10 Minutes

Reason for existing: Being available

The objective of careful sitting is to create consideration and nearness in the now, utilizing the breath as the object of core interest.

10. "Careful Meditation with Sam Harris"

Time: 9 Minutes

Intention: Being available

Thinker Sam Harris imparts to us this magnificent careful reflection, again centered around the breath and vibes of being available.

11. "Rest!"

Time: 10 Minutes

Reason: Relaxation for better rest

This is an extraordinary track in the event that you are experiencing difficulty nodding off around evening time. Joined with a binaural piece, it will help you rapidly unwind and enter a reflective state.

12. "Wake Up!"

Time: 10 Minutes

Reason: Starting the day

This track will assist you with kicking start your day with an astonishing vitality. This track was intended to assist you with imagining your day and satisfy your latent capacity, and it has a brainwave entrainment track that will assist you with arousing your mind and be alert.

CHAPTER FIFTEEN:
15 MINUTE GUIDED
RELAXATION

Contemplation practice frequently feels like something to get past, something bravo, similar to medication. However, as we become increasingly acquainted with rehearsing care, we can start to appreciate it as a chance to just be—to possess our body and be any place we are without doing anything specifically.

Clearly, there's nothing amiss with "doing" things— we need to get things done. Doing things is incredible, however, doing things is likewise testing. Having some time when we can simply be is invigorating.

No inquiry that just being is similarly as trying in light of the fact that some frightening musings may manifest. Be that as it may, as we become increasingly acquainted with the procedure, we understand we don't need to completely connect with those considerations or become involved with them.

In the event that it's an especially difficult time, the reflection practice will be tied in with being with that torment. We can enable it to be somewhat "spasmodic," that is, we see little holes in the torment where bits of unwinding, and euphoria even, can jab through.

Investigate This 15-Minute Guided Meditation

Set up Your Meditation Posture

The primary spot to begin is with investing a brief time of energy, in a casual way, on the stance.

We start with our seats. The point about our seat and our legs is simply to have a base, to be upheld. Nothing extraordinary about it.

- ❖ If you're on a seat: bottoms of the feet are contacting the ground.
- ❖ If you're on a pad: Legs can be essentially crossed before you or they could be in a lotus stance or half-lotus act.
- ❖ The chest area is upstanding however not hardened. Our hands can lay on our thighs before us with our upper arms parallel to our chest area.
- ❖ Our eyes can be open or shut, and our look is marginally down. Only a slight sentiment of humbleness about that. Furthermore, with the look down we're somewhat focussed internal. Our mouth can be simply somewhat open or shut.

Notice the Breath

Presently, basically, focus on your relaxing. Presently we focus on the breath as it comes in and goes out. The decent thing about the breath is that it's dependable. It's continually going to be there in case we're alive. Sharon Salzberg discusses the significance of confidence, numerous individuals talk about trust. It's an extremely basic sort of confidence or trust that something is going to keep on being there. As you end up out to lunch and you notice that since you have trust in the breath, you realize that it will be there when you bob off that idea and return to the breath.

Focus on the body and breathe together. As we return to and notice our breath, we're likewise seeing our body, so it's a sort of an entire body understanding, laying our consideration on the breath. We can likewise feel the temperature in the room and value our capacity to detect the world—that we are a tactile system. The world contacts us. We have an exchange going on with the world. That is something we can appreciate. Delight and torment originate from that detecting of the world.

Notice Thoughts and Emotions

For a brief period, work on coming back to the breath when the mind meanders. We're setting aside an effort to be available and to create nearness. Nearness meaning: ready to be available for whatever comes up—up or down, could be extremely exceptional contemplations.

How did the world start? For what reason would we say we are as yet driving such a significant number of autos? Who developed the vehicle in any case? How do vehicles work? It can be psychological, irregular musings like that. Or on the other hand, it could be extraordinary passionate considerations. Enthusiastic contemplations convey with them a ton of "shading," and a great deal of vitality, and a ton of sentiment of development in the body: "I loathe that," " love that,"— parts feeling tone to those musings. They can be tireless. They keep coming up, regardless of how frequently we return to the breath. Or then again, musings could be just about basic sensation it's a tingle in your toe.

Care is an equivalent open door process: whatever comes up, we simply notice it and return. In the event that it comes up again in another shape or structure, you know to sit and return. There's a sure measure of effortlessness and bluntness about that, however after some time that bluntness becomes normal unwinding. There's an inclination of solidarity that originates from having the option to be available with whatever emerges and not being so disposed to run from it.

A few people like to utilize the trademark "The present is wonderful," however that is not so much evident, fundamentally. The present can contain anything that is available at that time. In the event that a relative has simply kicked the bucket, it won't be especially lovely. Pausing for a minute to contemplate will be tied in with being with that, making an effort not to make a lovely encounter for yourself. Ordinarily, we're attempting to get something out of an encounter. For this situation, incomprehensibly, we are simply attempting to be with, instead of attempting to receive something in return.

As we notice contemplations over and over in reflection practice, the musings start to have less strong substance to them. They can feel less like something we need to battle with. We can have a thankfulness that they are not actualities, they're simply definitions that develop in the brain and that underneath them is some sort of essence and mindfulness that proceeds, whatever considerations may emerge and abide for some time and afterward go.

CHAPTER SIXTEEN: 20 MINUTE GUIDED RELAXATION

6 Effective 20-Minute Guided Meditations

1. Breathing Into Presence

Reason for existing: Being available and loose

This contemplation centers around the breath and how it very well may be your way to mindfulness and smoothness. It begins with a breathing exercise to quiet your sensory system, welcoming you into a loosening up perspective. You will be considerably more mindful of your environment and the sensations you are feeling in the present.

2. Adoring Kindness Meditation

Intention: Being available and loose

Like different reflections, the focal point of this track is being available and carefully mindful, with an accentuation on concentrating your expectations on adoration and consideration. This particular one doesn't have a foundation sound or music, yet the creator has a quieting and relieving voice if that is the thing that you are searching for.

3. Guided Meditation "Interfacing With The Calm Within"

Reason for existing: Being available and loose

This track by Diane Yeo is an incredible treat. Diane has a mitigating voice, and the track begins with a significant suggestion to enable your considerations to go back and forth. She likewise advises us that each experience is great and that there is nothing of the sort as a "terrible reflection."

4. Self-Care Meditation

Reason for existing: Being available and loose

This is an incredible track by Mary Mackley. You will see that this track is a piece of a digital recording with some more data on why it's essential to save space in your day for care and reflection as a self-care practice. The reason for this track is flawlessly lined up with the objective of this article — to give answers for your pressure and to assist you with having a progressively quick personal satisfaction just as a more advantageous perspective for the since quite a while ago run. Check this astonishing guided 20-minute reflection out!

5. The 6 Phase Meditation

Reason: Daily attestation for showing bounty in each part of your life

The 6 stages are an association, appreciation, opportunity from negative charges, inventive perception, expectations for the afternoon, and gift.

6. Care Meditation For Being Present

Reason for existing: Being available and loose

This is guided contemplation, composed and read by Sara Raymond, encourages you to build up your ability to be careful and present. It will decrease your feeling of anxiety, just as improve your general wellbeing and prosperity when rehearsed consistently.

Following stages with these guided 20-minute reflections

Presently you can begin destroying incessant worry from your life and grasping a training that — in addition to other things — will assist you with diminishing pressure, develop a solid cerebrum, and reinforce your mind-body association.

TIPS AND CONCLUSION

Contemplation was initially utilized for profound development, to turn out to be increasingly open to and mindful of the heavenly and the directing nearness of the sacred. Today, however, reflection has become a significant instrument in any event, for those individuals who don't think about themselves strict. It tends to be a wellspring of harmony and calm in a world that is truly ailing in both.

It very well may be utilized for recuperating, passionate purging and adjusting, extending fixation, opening imagination, and finding inward direction.

At the point when you start your contemplation, set your desires aside, and don't worry about the 'right' approach to do it. There are numerous approaches to think and there is no fixed models for deciding the right contemplation. What works for you is the correct strategy for you. Furthermore, discovering what works may require some experimentation and modifications. I list a number various methodologies beneath.

There are, be that as it may, a couple of things to keep away from when you start pondering:

Try not to attempt to compel something to occur.

Don't over-break down the reflection

Try not to attempt to make your mind clear or pursue considerations away

Keep in mind, there is nobody "right" approach to contemplate. Simply focus on the procedure and locate the most ideal route for YOU!

To begin thinking, pick a period and a spot where you won't be upset. That in itself may appear to be an outlandish errand. Except if you are a loner, there are most likely individuals throughout your life requesting your time and consideration.

You might need to tell these individuals that you will assist them with finding their socks, get the gum out of their hair, tune in to their tirades about the individuals at work, or whatever AFTER you've had a couple of moments of harmony and calm. Tell them this is something that you have to accomplish for yourself however they will likewise profit since you will be progressively loose, increasingly enthusiastic, and all the more adoring.

At the point when you are beginning, you just need 10 or 15 minutes for your contemplation session. This is a lot of time when you are starting and it likely could be this is constantly that you believe you can pry out of your bustling calendar for yourself. That is fine - it's vastly improved to put in almost no time a day contemplating than to put it off totally.

After some time, you may discover your reflection time so advantageous that you need to build the measure of time you spend in a thoughtful state. That is totally up to you. A decent objective is to work up to two brief reflection sessions every day. Research has demonstrated that investing this measure of energy contemplating prompts better wellbeing and can help decrease the anxieties and strains of day by day life.

The procedure is helped on the off chance that you can make it a propensity to contemplate at about a similar time every day. A few people find that thinking before anything else works for them. Others ruminate the last thing around evening time before resting. There is no specific time that is best for everybody. Whatever works for you is acceptable! Simply ensure that you practice all the time.

The real spot where you choose to think is again up to you. A couple of individuals put aside a room in their home as their reflection room however in case you're simply beginning, that is presumably a piece excessively outrageous. Rather, you may choose to contemplate in your room, the parlor, the kitchen or even the nursery - any place you are to the least extent liable to be upset. It is, obviously, better on the off chance that you don't attempt to reflect in the lounge while the remainder of the family is staring at the TV. Other than that the precise spot where you reflect doesn't make a difference - it's considerably more significant that you really start rehearsing contemplation.

In the event that you find that the first spot you picked isn't working for you, don't be hesitant to transform it. The equivalent goes for the time and the technique that you picked. A definitive advantage of reflection far surpasses the exact strategy for contemplation that you use to arrive at the advantage.

Perhaps the most straightforward approach to begin pondering is to utilize a guided reflection. The website www.soundstrue.com has numerous such guided symbolisms just as reflection music.

There are various kinds of reflection. We'll cover a portion of the more typical sorts beneath however on the off chance that none of these suit you, you'll find a lot more to investigate on the web. Don't hesitate to try different things with a portion of the various kinds of contemplation investigated beneath until you discover one that functions admirably for you.

Focusing

Focusing is a reflection in real life. Inside you is a space that is constantly quiet and settled. This space is frequently alluded to as your "quiet focus". Being focused methods staying in your quiet focus in the midst of the hecticness of regular daily existence. Being focused methods not enabling your inward light to be eclipsed by upsetting conditions or negative musings and feelings.

At the point when you are focused, you are in a condition of clearness, center, harmony, and equalization. At the point when you are not focused, you are hazy, unfocused, pushed, and wobbly.

A decent focusing strategy will require just insignificant consideration, enabling you to keep a portion of your consideration on the current movement, for example, washing dishes, collapsing clothing, or planting. Know, however, that your family might be more enticed to hinder in the event that they see you accomplishing something.

Simply disclose to them that you are additionally pondering and that except if they need to assist you with doing dishes, crease clothing, or nursery, they should disregard you for a couple of moments. Here are some fast in and out focusing strategies.

Basic Breath Awareness

While associated with anything that you are doing, carry some consideration regarding your relaxing for only a couple of seconds... it needn't be your complete consideration... sufficiently only to take you back to your quiet focus. Inhale normally, or maybe only somewhat more gradually and profoundly.

Recovering Your Energy

At the point when you are feeling pushed and dissipated, take a few moderate, full breaths. With each in-breath, envision you are pulling the entirety of your dispersed vitality and consideration back to your internal identity... your quiet focus.

Giving up

This focusing method joins breath mindfulness with the expression or mantra, "Let go." It is particularly useful when you are tense as well as focusing on an unpleasant circumstance or a negative idea or feeling.

As you breathe in, state (quietly or so anyone might hear), "Let". As you breathe out, say "go"... while relinquishing all that is focusing on you.

Unwinding Meditation

This astoundingly simple and loosening up contemplation utilizes somewhat known mystery about the eyes. Enabling the eyes to rest in a delicate descending look has a moment, programmed loosening up impact.

Unwinding contemplation gives a lot of pressure to decrease and can be utilized as a snappy 2 moment unwind and revive break anyplace (yet not while driving). You will likewise understand an increased feeling of readiness.

Sit easily with your spine sensibly straight.

Enable your eyes to rest easily descending, looking delicately, however not concentrated on anything.

Without shutting your eyes totally, let your eyelids drop to a level that feels generally great.

Keep looking descending... the demonstration of looking is your essential center (as opposed to the region at which you are looking). You may see your breathing getting progressively cadenced.

It's OK to let your consideration float a piece. In the event that your eyes become overwhelming, it's OK to allow them to close.

In the event that you notice you've left your casual space, just take your consideration back to your casual descending look.

Breathing Meditation

In this contemplation, you will concentrate on your breath. This is presumably perhaps the least demanding technique for reflection in the first place.

Start by embracing an agreeable position. At the point when you sit to think, sit easily, with your spine sensibly straight. This enables the otherworldly vitality to stream unreservedly up the spine, which is a significant part of reflection. Inclining toward a seat back, a divider, headboard, and so on is splendidly good. On the off chance that, for physical reasons, you can't sit up, lay level on your back. Spot your hands in any position that is agreeable.

When you're agreeable, close your eyes.

Begin to see your relaxing. We inhale so frequently that we will, in general, underestimate relaxing. So set aside the effort to see your relaxing.

Notice the air filling your lungs.

At that point notice as you inhale out and the air leaves your lungs. Rehash the way toward seeing your breath.

As you do this, you'll discover considerations coming up. They may be about family, companions, work or totally whatever else. That doesn't make a difference - it's everything part of the procedure and it is consummately ordinary to keep on having considerations while you are contemplating.

Be that as it may, when these contemplations come up, let them float out with your next breath. Each time your musings float, take your psyche back to concentrating on your relaxing.

Strolling Meditation

In the event that you think that its hard to sit still and keep your eyes shut while reflecting, at that point strolling contemplation could be beneficial for you.

There are four parts to a mobile contemplation:

Getting mindful of your relaxing

Seeing your environment

Being cognizant and mindful to your body's development

Setting aside some effort to think about your contemplation experience

Become mindful of your taking similarly as you would for the breathing reflection process. Notice every breath as you take in and afterward inhale out once more.

Become aware of the air filling your lungs and utilize every exhalation to convey any diverting considerations.

At the point when you start seeing your environment, you'll likely be flabbergasted. We underestimate loads of things in our regular daily existence and a lot of what is around us goes totally unnoticed. At the point when you are strolling near, notice the various hues that you see.

Don't simply see hues. Tune in for sounds. There might be feathered creature tune, street clamor or the jabber of individuals or creatures. Intentionally check out these various sounds. Notice the various tunes sung by the feathered creatures.

On the off chance that you are in an urban region, focus on the distinctive traffic clamors. Every's motor sounds somewhat unique. So does the sound of wheels on the distinctive road surfaces. You'll wind up hearing things that have just passed you by previously.

There are likewise scents to fill your faculties. Perhaps the fragrance of newly mown grass or the sweet smell that happens soon after a shower of a downpour. There are a lot of scents in the climate and the odds are that a large portion of these has slipped past your cognizance.

Tune into your body's development. Begin to see the lightweight on the bottoms of your feet as you walk. Know about the artificially glamorizing your skin, regardless of whether it's a quiet day or a blustery one. Focus on your body's development as you stroll around. Feel how your arms swing. Notice how you hold your head - is it upstanding and mindful or an alternate position? Change your thoughtfulness regarding diverse body parts as you are strolling and you'll be entranced at what you find.

When you've finished your strolling reflection, set aside a limited quantity of effort to return to your ordinary world. During this period, intellectually go through your considerations and sentiments that you encountered during your contemplation time. Figure what you can do to improve your experience much further next time you decide to do a mobile reflection.

Step by step return from your tranquil site to your standard world.

All-inclusive Mantra Meditation

This contemplation originates from an old Indian book called the MaliniVijayaTantra, which goes back around 5000 years. It is a simple reflection, yet extremely ground-breaking in its ability to calm your mind and associate you with your Essence or Inner Spirit.

This contemplation utilizes a mantra as your object of core interest. A mantra is a word or expression that has the ability to catalyze a move into more profound, increasingly tranquil conditions of mindfulness. The mantra most use for this contemplation is Aum. Aum doesn't have a strict interpretation. Or maybe, it is the basic vibration of the universe. If you somehow managed to tune into the real solid of the universe, the unending sound of "Aummm" is the thing that you would hear.

In spite of the fact that this mantra is here and there recited so anyone might hear, in this contemplation, you will rehash the mantra intellectually... quietly.

Before we get to the genuine strides, there are a couple of significant focuses to know about:

One of the keys to this reflection is rehashing the mantra tenderly or faintly in your brain.

The intensity of this procedure originates from giving up and enabling your thoughtfulness regarding plunge into the more profound domains of mindfulness.

In this manner, despite the fact that you will concentrate on the mantra, remaining concentrated on the mantra isn't the point of this reflection.

Making a decent attempt to remain centered would prevent your consideration from slipping into the more profound domains. Rather, you will rehash the mantra with "insignificant exertion", and giving your mind the space to meander a piece.

Oppose the impulse to get something going, and enable the mantra to take the necessary steps.

This reflection effectively creates a move into more profound, increasingly tranquil conditions of mindfulness. (The level of this will differ from session to session.) It expands the progression of vitality to the cerebrum and cleans up a decent arrangement of physical and passionate poisons.

In view of this detoxification, it is ideal to hold this contemplation to 10 or 15 minutes every day when initially starting. Following a month or something like that, it tends to be expanded to 20 minutes, however, that ought to be the most extreme for any individual who doesn't have many long periods of contemplation experience. Likewise, it is prudent to drink a great deal of unadulterated water.

At last, mantra contemplation quickens profound development as you accomplish a condition of unwinding and mindfulness.

Sit easily, with your eyes shut and your spine sensibly straight.

Start rehashing the mantra tenderly in your brain.

Rehash the mantra at whatever beat feels generally common. There is no compelling reason to synchronize the mantra with your breathing, however on the off chance that this happens normally, it's alright.

Enable the mantra to emerge all the more faintly in your brain... rehashing it with insignificant exertion.

Keep rehashing the mantra faintly, and consider whatever occurs.

In the event that whenever you feel that you are slipping into rest like or dream-like state, enable it to occur.

On the off chance that and when you notice that your consideration has floated totally off the mantra, delicately start rehashing it, and proceed with negligible exertion.

Following 10 or 15 minutes, quit rehashing the mantra, and leave your contemplation gradually.

After any contemplation strategy, permit yourself a minute to relish the feeling of skimming and quiet that encompasses you. Take a full breath, brace your flanks (allegorically), and adventure forward into your day by day adjusts with restored vitality and a profound feeling of harmony.

CPSIA information can be obtained
at www.ICGtesting.com
Printed in the USA
LVHW021020291220
675197LV00001B/150

9 781801 142277